From Dawn 'til Dusk - A Farmer's Nature Journal
S Taylor

Slippery Jacks Press

From Dawn 'til Dusk - A Farmer's Nature Journal
Copyright © S Taylor 2015

Illustrations copyright © J.L. Tolmie

ISBN 978-0-9926648-7-9

First published 2015 by Slippery Jacks Press

Acknowledgements

Thank you to Carol, Rob, Owain and Liz – we're a team!
Thanks to Robin, Bina and my Hazelwood companions for showing me these observations were worth publishing.

Thank you to Janie for your work on the illustrations – seeing my words come to life in your drawing was such a thrill.
And thank you to Slippery Jacks for putting it all together.

Foreword

Rather than a day to day diary of life on an organic dairy farm this book is a compilation of my experiences and interactions with nature as I move through the farming year, the sorts of things that make a farmer look up from his work and say "Aah, this is the life!"

My patch of land is by no means pristine unbroken countryside – we are bordered by two main roads, a town and a village and yet the community of animals and plants described here manage to thrive. I think this is a testament to the resilience of Nature – she only needs the space and opportunity to weave her tapestry of life.

A traditional livestock farm with its trees, hedgerows and copses is woven into that tapestry, living and working in this environment perhaps gives me an advantage in observing the other threads in the warp and weft of the countryside. The American ecologist Aldo Leopold wrote of what the farmer may see in his cow pasture – these pages are my record of what I have seen.

Stuart Taylor
Argoed October 2015

January

1st

The overnight rain has left everything engulfed by moisture – the relative humidity must be 100%! There is a cloudbank filling the valley, following the course of the river. Although there are patches of blue sky the cloud to the east means that the sun's rays can only escape in places but where they strike the valley cloud they illuminate it as if it were neon gas. Later the sun climbs above the cloud and manages to brighten everything, making the droplets of water on the hedgerows shine.

At dinner time I was amused to see a group of fifteen fat, grey woodpigeons foraging in the paddock in front of the house. Waddling around scratching for seeds amongst the grass they looked like a flock of hens.

2nd

Noticed a very dark cock pheasant sitting on the rails in front of the house so erectly with his tail vertically downwards that he looks like a parrot or some other exotic jungle fowl.

3rd

This morning as I milked the cows I was able to see the moon rising through the open parlour door. It was obscured by the dark silhouette of the farm-house to begin with but gradually rose behind the bare tree branches into the clear predawn sky accompanied by an attendant 'star' (so bright I think it must have been a planet, probably Venus). Just recently the moon is brighter than normal - apparently it is closer than usual. The crescent and star climbed higher as the dark sky lightened to the blue of dawn, a gradual unfolding of choreographed beauty.

4th

Providing enough firewood to heat a large farmhouse is hard work and time consuming and I sometimes wish we had it easy with gas or oil heating and yet I cannot imagine not gathering firewood – at least it is an excuse to spend a couple of hours in the wood!

After the tree has been felled I cut it into three foot lengths and then split it lengthways with iron wedges. These force the timber apart along the natural contours of the wood. It sometimes seems that I am dissecting a leviathan in order to inspect the inner structures of a mighty body. Here there is a line of rot running down the centre of the tree, or here a localised area where the tree has lost a branch. I once found a nine inch metal peg completely en-closed inside the flesh of the tree presumably driven in decades ago and since enveloped by the growing tree.

5th

Sunday evening 7pm - it is a clear and frosty night, the new moon has risen and set already, peeping through the trees into the cowshed as we finished milking. Orion is rising in the east, starting his climb across the dark canopy of the night sky. Woodsmoke from our chimney flows northwards against the starry ceiling. There is a feeling that everything is in place for some happening that will take place in the many dark hours before dawn tomorrow. Humans have retreated from the cold into our warm houses leaving the night to the dark and its creatures.

6th

Saw the heron on the middle of a field apparently eating something that was almost too big and having to put it down to get a better grip before swinging it up and with a certain backwards throw of the head dispatching it down his sinuous neck. Hope it wasn't one of my moorhens!

7th

I like to grow crab apples from pips every few years and plant them out for the sheer beauty of the blossom in spring and as a source of fruit for the wildlife. This afternoon I took the pips out of the crabs I collected in the autumn, half splitting them with a knife and then tearing them open to avoid cutting the valuable seeds. The greenhouse was soon filled with the sweet fruity smell of apples. I was tempted enough to try tasting a portion of the flesh but found it as sour as any crab apple on the tree.

8th

I was supposed to be going to a farm meeting today that was cancelled, leaving me with a packed lunch to use up so I went and had a picnic in the dingle despite the north wind. I found a place in the lee of an oak tree with a view of the stream running away to the south west. The main vegetation at this time of year was ivy, growing up the tree next to me with hairy stems two to three inches thick giving it the appearance of a liana in a tropical rainforest. The floor was also covered with a carpet of ivy mixed with old sycamore leaves marked with the black spots of the fungus that signifies good air (because air pollution inhibits its growth). Even now there are promises of spring – fool's parsley and red campion leaves poking up out of the leaf litter. It was cold though – my hands were purple by the time I finished eating!

9th

Started restoring a hedge that has got too big for the hedgecutter. It grows along the edge of the wood against a line of Scots pine trees. Because of the lack of light down at ground level there is no vegetation, all the growth is up at the top of the hedge fifteen feet above. Somehow it has the air of a dusty forgotten passage in a gothic mansion or cathedral – the trunks of the trees are like the columns and the hedge stems like lesser struts and beams arching up to meet the main structure.

10th

Noticed a pile of shelled rosehips – mostly the flesh but some seeds on top of a timber gatepost. The pile was eight inches by four and one inch deep in the middle, probably the work of a squirrel.

11th

The mornings are still dark but the evenings are beginning to draw out "by a gnat's yawn". After a couple of days of rain at 4pm today there was some blue sky and pink clouds. The moon in its second quarter was high in the east, sometimes hidden and sometimes free of the clouds. It was still half light at 5pm.

12th

A flock of about forty wild geese came from the north west, only just clearing the beech trees behind the house. They were flying in an uneven V formation, one arm having three times as many birds as the other (something to do with air currents I wonder?).
About twenty minutes later a smaller group passed in the same direction – perhaps the missing birds of the flock trying to catch up!

13th

The weather was strange this morning. Yesterday was a really wet day, pools of water appearing in the fields; water running off the fields through gates onto the concrete drive so that this morning it was a relief to go out to a clear starry sky. By eight am there was ice on water standing in the wheel barrow and the post box door had frozen shut but the yard's concrete was wet not frozen. It must have been the air that was freezing but the ground had enough residual warmth to keep the surface frost free. As I write this at one pm the sun is shining strongly through the window, warming my shoulder. A very different day to yesterday.

14th

The first real frost this morning. The air is grey with cold mist, the hollies have whitened leaves, brown oak and beech leaves cling to the younger trees and skeletal briars trail out from the hedges, fawn coloured and barbed. I put some peanuts out for the birds, frost can be a nuisance for us but it is surely life or death for a small bird that has struggled through a cold night. The feeders hang from the monkey puzzle tree in the garden. Having filled them I then gave the dogs some milk and passed the garden gate not two minutes later and there were three birds on the feeders – they must keep a hopeful watch. Later on I passed again and although there were no birds the feeders were turning around and around on their axis, so the birds must have left as I approached.

15th
The evenings are beginning to get lighter now and tonight was especially pleasant. There was a breeze from the west and the birds were singing. I wish that I could adequately describe the subtle changes in weather and light that define each day and night.

It is always good to see the new moon for the first time each month, so slender in the blue dark of the south west sky. I usually notice it while I am doing the routine evening jobs of feeding and scraping out, just above the shelter belt of Scots pine trees that surround the western edge of the farmyard and above the yellow lights of the town down in the valley. Already past its zenith and beginning to set it will be gone when I go out later to look around the cows before going to bed.

16th
The tractor hedgecutter cannot cut right up to any tree that might be growing in the hedge and so there are always one or two stems of hedge species that will grow on if not cut back by hand which I admit does not always get done. I noticed today a holly stem two to three inches thick that has succeeded in reaching ten feet up the trunk of an oak tree where it has met the first branch and followed the underside of it so that the two of them arch gracefully outwards towards the field.

17th
The stream in the dingle has over the years exposed a substantial root of an oak tree growing on the bank. The root is now over the centre of the stream and extends almost fifteen feet along the length of the water before returning to the bank. There is a six inch wide crack with rounded, healed bark along its sides and in the centre of the fissure grow two male ferns – a yard above the water. Upstream a dogwood branch has collapsed and folded down to the stream and colonies of bracket fungus grow on the weakened wood.

18th

Very windy at lunch time today. It has broken two skylights on the cow shed and strewn small branches of Scots pine and strands of ivy ripped from the trees across the yard. We have a Californian redwood growing behind the farmhouse that has had branches two inches thick torn off it and deposited fifty yards away in the field, luckily passing over the power line that supplies the farm without damaging it. A Denbigh plum tree has had its top broken, the tree has only produced one or two fruits in recent years but I am sorry to see it snapped in two.

In the wood there is an old multi stemmed holly that has lost one of its trunks – about a foot thick at the base. A large Scots pine has blown over and is bending the top of one of the young oak trees, another two are leaning over as are four larches in the plantation on the other side of the drive.

19th

A grey, dreary evening when I went out to milk – slushy snow on the wind but I happened to look round at the trees to the east of the yard and saw that the sun was picking out a larch still clothed in its dead needles and shining copper in the weak sunlight while next to it a spruce tree shone green. A welcome splash of colour on a grey day.

20th

I was working in the wood getting firewood at dusk as the full moon rose over the village, appearing very large behind and between the houses. There was just enough cloud to seem to be wrapped around that ball of white light. It soon cleared the houses and cloud and by the time I drove back to the yard it was high above the fields. Later on there was a slight mist which made the moonlight soft and diffuse giving a more ethereal effect than normal.

21st

I was more tired than usual this morning when I got up for milking at five am but when I stepped out of the front door the weather was so pleasant I instantly felt refreshed and glad to be alive. The wind was strong but mild, coming from the west, high cloud drifted over the yard. Once again I felt that the night had been a magical time but that I had missed it by being tucked up safely in bed (not that I am prepared to forgo a nights sleep – cows have to be milked!). It was a shame to be stuck in the parlour milking instead of wandering the fields in the predawn darkness.

22nd
Noticed from a distance a dried out thistle plant on top of the slope in one of the fields, buffeted by the breeze, bending to one side, straightening and being bent over again repeatedly – how lonely and blasted it looked.

23rd
A very windy afternoon, by 6.30pm the wind had snapped the top off a Grand fir behind the yard – a length eight yards long and nine inches in diameter at the point of the break. The tip of the tree was broken off about three feet down and then another section two feet long before the main body that now lies broken and forlorn in the field. I am sad to see it brought low – I used to climb it when I was a boy.

24th
I was struck by how serene the pond looks, as still as glass reflecting the sky above.

25th
I am often struck by the determination of the birds to sing. This morning I could hear them above the radio while still in bed. When I went out I found that it was a grey, dark and damp morning.

26th
This morning it is so calm that even the aspens are completely still and quiet. The gales of yesterday and the rest of the week are gone. Yesterday morning two hen pheasants were perched on the rails of a tree enclosure in the paddock. The wind was ruffling the feathers on their sides and seemed to threaten to use the leverage of their long tail feathers to turn them around and off the rail but they stayed there, perhaps enjoying the challenge. The wind at times was bending the mature Sitka spruce trees and I wondered that they did not break.

Tonight there is a full moon high in the eastern sky; a stationary layer of white cloud is so high it appears close to the moon. Lower down, pinkish brown clouds move across the sky.

27th
The first snow of the winter this morning - about an inch of a very wet and soft snow.

This afternoon a freezing wind from the north picked up and it snowed again. Ice built up on the latches and hinges of gates like a crustaceous growth on a ship wreck, completely covering the latches and making it necessary to chip the crystalline growth away in order to open the gate.

28th
Quite a heavy fall of snow this evening. It is the full moon so when I came out to look around about 8.30pm I walked into a winter wonderland. The sky was clear and sharp, the tree branches dusted with snow and all illuminated so brightly by moonlight that bounced back off the snow as well as falling from above. The paddock and beech trees by the pond were particularly beautiful – they looked as if made of crystal, the whole scene looked pristine.

29th
Found a piece of dried and pressed gorse in the hay when I swept up after moving some wads of a bale. It was dried to the same bluey green colour as the hay and about the size and shape of a lucky sprig of heather. It must have been young growth torn off the hedge by the machine as we turned the hay last summer as it was not prickly at all. I eventually dropped it in with the hay, thinking of how the old timers would mill gorse to feed to livestock.

30th
Yesterday was wet and windy, becoming very windy last night so it was a pleasure to step out of the door this morning to a calm clear sky. It is hard to believe that the moon that peeped so tentatively through the trees two weeks ago is now so dominant in the night sky, throwing very sharp shadows, creating triangles and trapezoids of light where it strikes the walls of the loose boxes over the doors. On the yard which is drying out after the rain the moonlight makes silver traceries out of the meandering patches of damp that remain. It strikes me that this magical light is all the more welcome at this time of year when there is so little daylight.

31st
A month gone already! Today I cut the hedge along the drive to a very formal pointed "A" shape - almost topiary. There is something refreshing about a newly cut hedge, the sharp edge along the top is very satisfying. It is amazing how a couple of feet off the top increases the view beyond and lets the light in. It makes the place look organised and cared for.

The hedges are very important to me. They are like ribbons of wildwood weaving their way across the tamed farmland. In their depths, at the bottom and centre lies the old wood where you can still see how they were laid decades ago. The hands that crafted the hedge are gone but the craftwork remains. Dead leaves and berries, discarded thorns and occasional rails of fencing lie on the ground beneath the canopy. Briars thread their way through the younger growth higher up. Later on in the year all this will be swamped by exuberant herbaceous growth, wild flowers and the fresh green leaves of the hawthorn itself.

February

1st

I have been thinking this morning how the everchanging weather conditions – the interplay of light, rain, wind and temperature are the variables that we notice and how the stimulus for most of the entries in this journal are all external aspects of nature. There must also be a vast range of internal conditions, ever changing and interacting, an internal milieu i.e. sugars and chemicals in plants and trees, varying movements of water and nutrients, pH changes and electrical changes right down to cellular level. A vast ebb and flow, a pulsating tide of life activities hidden to even the most observant naked eye.

2nd

Ground conditions are very wet now. We had an inch of snow last week which thawed and was followed by a weekend of wind and rain. There are pools of water at the side of the drive and in the field gateways. However it was still a surprise to find a frog in the milking parlour pit as I cleaned the clusters after milking! A yellowish adult, I suppose looking for a breeding pond at this time of year.

3rd

A breezy, grey morning with a "red sky in the morning" that illuminated the underside of the clouds, picking out their contours and giving them a solid looking texture. The reflected light was shining on the walls of the buildings as if a light had been left on.

4th

Admired the green Scots pine foliage against a frosty blue sky and the warm glow of sunlight on the reddish brown bark. I noticed the ash trees in the new plantation catching the sun but looking as pale and insubstantial as a layer of mist, ghostly against the backdrop of the darker coloured sycamores behind.

5th

Found tiny one dimensional ice formations on the tractor windscreen. They must have been small drops of moisture that had frozen to form delicate structures that looked like snowflakes, as soon as I drove into the sunshine they melted away.

6th

As I was milking this evening I noticed two crows sitting in the snow covered branches of the beech trees behind the house. They looked like dark, witchy ornaments set on the sugarcrafted icing of a cake.

Later on the orangey white glow of a snow filled sky merged with the snow covered roofs of the farm buildings so that it was impossible to see where the roof ended and the sky began.

7th

One of the farm tasks that is most distasteful to me is catching moles. I have nothing against the little creatures but their hills put soil in the silage which spoils the fermentation and can even be a source of disease for the cows. Apparently they are basically woodland creatures that venture out to grassland, if only they would stop in the woods.

I wonder what it is like down there in their subterranean world, a network of twisting and turning tunnels, some of them major highways – deep, broad and well worn and some of them meandering lanes that lead nowhere. I remember in school reading a piece in an English lesson about the world of moles that mentioned the thud of hares gambolling overhead. Anyway, to get back to the point – yesterday I caught the first mole of the season and it was an albino! - A bit of a shock. Presumably he did not suffer any prejudice from his fellows, how would they know he was a different colour down there in the dark?

8th

Passed a stand of burdock plants in the wood that were dried out and brown but looking very architectural almost like lightstands of art nouveau scroll work, their branches bending gracefully and the clusters of burrs on the end of each branch. I am sure I did not brush against a plant, only pass within their orbit but when I looked down at my sleeve there were three burrs attached – can they jump?

9th

A very windy day, the pond surface is far from serene today – a constant stream of ripples move along its length and whenever there is an extra gust of wind a disturbance shoots across the whole grey sheet like a digital pictogram changing.

10th

I went to look at the boiler before milking this morning and so was round the back of the house earlier than normal and was rewarded with the sight of the waning moon before it had risen over the house roof. It was great to see it so low in the sky shining on the pond, giving its reflection to the surface whether or not there was someone there to see it. An hour later it had risen over the house and a small fluffy cloud appeared to be held within its crescent.

11th

This morning we have been pruning the lower side branches from the oak trees we planted a few years ago. Hopefully this will prevent climbing weeds from clinging to the branches and scrambling up the tree. It is strange to think that these trees will barely have reached their prime long after I am dead and gone. Tree planting is probably the longest lasting memorial you can leave behind you. Two centuries from now no one will remember me but these oaks that I planted should still be here. Further, if one succeeds to farm well, to live a good life and not harm others and achieve the lesser targets that our society makes so much of – make money or in agriculture achieve a certain return or yield or come up to some bench mark, all these things fall apart on our deaths but with luck the trees that we successfully established will go on for centuries and may turn out to be the most worthwhile thing we did in our entire lives.

12th

A cold morning (-6C). Surprised to see four carrion crows stalking around the yard, the need for food having driven them to it, they do not usually come in the yard.

13th

I spent a very pleasant afternoon hedgelaying today. Having just seen the film "What Dreams May Come" where the central premise is that each soul creates its own heaven it occurred to me that my heaven might be a moment from this afternoon enjoyed for evermore – the golden sunshine in the bright clear air of the first promise of spring, withered brown leaves rattling in the cold breeze and complete absorption and satisfaction in an activity.

14th

Cutting a hedge and looking against the sun as it rose in a clear sky I could see clouds of frost particles being thrown off the hedge by the machine.

15th

I had my afternoon cuppa sitting on the front door porch step with two dogs and a cat. The sky was clear and blue and the setting sun shone through the rough and knobbled branches of the bare fruit trees in the paddock.

16th

After a couple of days of hard frost it has now turned wet. It is very strange to be walking through rain but feeling the fields rock hard beneath my feet.

17th

When I opened the parlour door to let the first cows out this morning I noticed the crescent moon behind the chimney stack of the house. The crescent itself was hidden by the stack which was a black silhouette against the diffused glow of moonlight. Two hours later the moon was directly overhead in the south, riding in a sky of blue and pink bands.

In the afternoon I was sitting underneath my favourite oak tree watching the dog running around and playing with one of his beloved sticks. A cock pheasant ran from somewhere, disturbed by our presence. The dog dropped his stick and stared, ears cocked and spellbound doing nothing as the pheasant disappeared into the distance. Then he went back to his stick – some hunter!

18th

One night before the full moon and the moon is illuminating a foggy night. The trees loom overhead in the opaque air, everything is still and the streetlights of the road are blotted out by the all encompassing grey.

19th

Noticed a wood pigeon trying to eat the berries of a big clump of ivy growing on the garage. The vegetation was not strong enough to take his weight and he kept sinking into the shiny green foliage, sometimes up to his neck and would have to flap his way back to the surface, eventually giving up and flying off. He may have been disappointed anyway – the berries are not ripe yet, still green not black.

20th

The birds are starting to think of spring – I hear the owls hooting when I go to look round about 8.30 pm and this morning there was a woodpecker knocking somewhere in the trees behind the house.

21st

Looking down the lane from the yard, the late afternoon sunshine was lighting the brown coloured hedgerow oaks, the whole scene seemed to be in sepia tints.

22nd

Cutting the hedge along the wood. I went in the wood to cut off stems I could not reach with the tractor from the field. Even though it is a north facing slope there are bluebell leaves two to three inches tall growing in the shelter of the hedge and trees.

23rd
The moon, Jupiter and Venus are in alignment with the moon in the south and the two planets to the west.

24th
On my neighbours field there is a medium sized oak tree growing out of a stump that has been cut off in the past about knee height. The upper surface of the stump is about three feet in diameter and so must have been old when cut, and now it has regrown another tree older than anyone alive now to see it – how far back that oak must go!

25th
Hedgecutting in the back field that adjoins my neighbour's wood. The oak trees seemed to be stretching their fingery branches through the perimeter hedge as if jealous of the cultivated fields, like prisoners reaching their hands through cell bars.

26th
Went for a walk amongst the young trees that were planted on the bypass embankment fifteen years ago. I had wanted to walk along the top of the bank between the trees and the hedge but it was too overgrown so I went half way down the slope where there is a shelf a vehicle's width with a French drain running centrally. There was less vegetation on the gravel so it was natural to follow it like a path but at one point there is a fifteen foot alder growing in it so I had to sidestep that to continue. The trees are mainly broadleaves – ash, oak with last year's brown leaves still clinging, alder with its dried fruits, rowans and here and there the occasional evergreen of Scots pine and holly. Eventually I reached the underside of the bridge that carries a road over the bypass and returned over the fence to our trackway.

27th
Found a hollow in the wood that forms a sort of natural amphitheatre. There is a stump of a sycamore felled a few years ago that has bracket fungus growing out of it looking as if someone has thrown plates that have embedded in it. The whole stump and fungal structures are covered in moss. The place seems to be a particularly wet spot in this generally wet small wood, even some wild

raspberry canes have six inches of moss growing up their smooth stems.

28th
Noticed an old bird's nest from last year, a goblet of moss and larch needles built in an elder bush. Growing on the flat top was a nice clump of cleavers, fresh and green four feet above the ground.

March

1st
Will the daffodils be out for St David's day? – only in the mildest and earliest of springs here. The first ones to flower are a group that grow at the base of a sycamore stump that perhaps gives them a sheltered micro climate. The main group in the garden and paddock are always a few days later. These original

plantings have a double buttery yellow flower. There are others that were planted around the wildlife pond and on its island with paler petals and darker coloured trumpets.

2nd
Noticed that some of the young trees on the embankment along the bypass have been snapped off by the wind.

3rd
Saw the first bumblebee of the year as I was crossing the farmyard this morning. It came winging its way along in that zigzag slightly drunken looking flight they have to within about six feet of me and then turned back the way it had come, almost as if it was just saying hello.

4th
The birds were singing as I milked this morning and a robin came in the parlour and sang very loudly, drowning out the sounds of pulsation and cows knocking feeders – a most acceptable payment for the crumb of cow food he pinches each day.

5th
Although the temperature was as low as 1.2C when I went out of the house this morning it seemed positively balmy compared to the recent frost. The snow covered roofs seemed almost luminous against the starry sky.

6th
Noticed a large cock pheasant very close to the house and by standing back from the window I was able to watch him without him seeing me. It was the closest I have ever been to a live pheasant, only six feet away with the glass between us. It was a chance to admire his colours and poise as he strutted about with his long tail feathers floating out behind him.

7th
As I was getting firewood out of the woodstore I heard a loud buzzing and saw a bumblebee flying around, perhaps I had disturbed her. The body seemed very big compared to the wings, she flew around for a while as if checking what I was up to before flying out through the door.

8th
After a cold blustery day the sky cleared completely by evening, the air was very cold and clear as a heron flew over the yard.

9th
After a cold, grey drizzly day yesterday, this morning was surprisingly clear and frosty minus 4C in fact. There was a glorious dawn, the sky lightening to a crystal clear blue with rays of sunshine striking the yard and buildings horizontally before 7am. Five geese flew over from the north, their cries carrying through the cold air. In the afternoon the sunny spells alternated with snow showers, so much so that when I went into one building it was sunny and clear skied, I came out five minutes later into a blizzard – the sky completely grey and large snowflakes being driven by the wind.

10th
Noticed a large flock of seagulls circling in a loose vortex against the backdrop of a dark bank of cloud, the birds in front catching the light and then receding as they moved around to the back. Occasionally they would separate into a pattern resembling the double helix of DNA, all the time rotating in the sky and then move back to the original shape.

11th
The predawn sky was well lit this morning – a red sky towering in the east, the rest of the firmament blue and the last quarter of the moon shining white in the west.

12th
Three inches of snow this morning. I had to put the snow plough on the tractor and just finished clearing the drive in time for the milk tanker to collect the milk. The snow has slipped down the roofs making a feathered edge like the neatly trimmed eaves of a thatched roof.

13th
Set up a bumblebee nest box I have bought. When I went to get some soil to cover the entrance pipe I saw a large black coloured bee investigating a nearby pile of stones for nesting – there is a lesson there!

14th
Venus (I think) is shining brightly in the western sky above the pines that form

a shelter belt on that side of the yard. It follows a shallow arc and is setting in the north west by 9pm.

15th
Noticed four cock pheasants strutting about together at the top of one of the fields.

16th
It is wet and misty today but we have had a few days of dry spring like weather this week.   The land has dried up and I have been trying to catch up with the fieldwork. There are two cock pheasants strolling around regally in a sort of bumbling, nosy way. Yesterday one of them ambled across the line of the tractor as I was spreading slurry, apparently interested in what was going on and determined not to panic and fly – just walking past.   The carrion crows are thinking about nesting, they can be seen in pairs, sleek and blue-black, flapping off gates with a surprisingly large wingspan carrying likely nesting material.   I saw two March hares gambolling back and to over a bare patch of cop in a gap in one of the hedges.

17th
Saw a heron flying over the cow shed, so slowly that that it seemed to be hovering, the sunlight illuminating its underside against the blue March sky.

18th
Disturbed four or five snipe on a field where I was spreading slurry and then another on a different field later on. I have never seen so many in one day, normally I see one or at the most two. How wildly they fly when startled – not like the lazy, indolent flapping of the crows.

19th
Delighted to see a bumblebee visiting the flowers of a potted snakes head fritillary that we've only just bought. She would fly up into the drooping heads, disappearing completely and then reappear with a dusting of pollen on her back between the wings and enter another flower. She then flew off in her curious zigzag way – can't they fly straight at all?

20th
Noticed some dead ivy leaves blown into a row on the straw at the front of a loosebox looking like an ornament made of sheet bronze.

21st

Scavenging for firewood in the wood towards the northern edge by the road. There is a good area of lords and ladies growing green and strong, some plain green and some mottled or maculatum as the botanic name specifies. The dog's mercury is coming on as well also a patch of wood anemone two metres radius in flower. A wide area of bluebell leaves under the two main oak trees.

22nd

There is a copse of Scots pine behind the yard that is gradually being colonised by broadleaved trees such as oak and beech. The trees are about five feet high and being young have kept their brown leaves all winter, looking picturesque even though at this time of year I am eager to see new green foliage. There is some hawthorn just about to break open, the swollen light coloured buds almost seem to glow in comparison to the grey sky.

23rd

The damson tree is covered in blossom. Seen against the dull grey sky it is like a canopy of faery lights illuminating the garden path.

24th

Cutting the ivy out of the gutters on the front of the house. Some of it has grown two feet up the slates of the roof, trapped underneath were dry, brown beech leaves that floated up on the air currents looking like butterflies.

25th

We are told that early woodland plants such as primrose and wood anemone have evolved to grow and flower before the canopy of tree leaves closes and shades the floor of the wood, but I wonder to what extent individual plants can learn the same idea? I thought about this today when I went to examine the hedge along the back of the farmyard. It is shaded by two oak trees and a beech. I was surprised to find it well advanced in leaf when the other hedges are slower (except the younger hedges which are always first into leaf). Has this row of hawthorns learnt to come into leaf as early as possible so as to get some growth on before they are shaded by the trees?

26th

Such a heavy white frost on the fields and roofs that when I went to get a bucket of water from the rain barrel there was a continuous trickle of drips from the downspout – the frost melting as the sun shone on the roofs.

27th

Yesterday the cock and hen pheasant were in the paddock in front of the house. We have put a mixture of chaff, small broken grains and weed seeds (rejects from grain cleaning) underneath the fir trees for the birds. The cock was easily seen, puffing out his chest, showing off his colours he reminded me of Henry the eighth in all his regalia. The hen was much less conspicuous, muted browns and fawns almost the same colour as the piles of seeds. How secretive she is, it is almost unusual to see a hen pheasant whereas her mate is seen almost every day at this time of year. The way that he walks - bumbling, eccentric – "ahh! Whats going on here?" his manner seems to say, puts me in mind of the very class that hunts him – the stereotype of a fat country squire in a tweed suit with a waistcoat that is distastefully colourful.

28th

I was amused to see some wagtails congregating around a water trough in one of the fields. First two alighted on the rim, then another two and then another two that landed on the rail above and then hopped down to join the others.

29th

I finally finished ploughing tonight, exactly five months after starting. That is how long the wet weather has held us up. Rain was forecast the next day so I carried on until 8.30 by which time it was going dark, there were spots of rain on the tractor windscreen as I put the plough away after finishing, now that is the definition of satisfaction! As it went dark I felt once again something I have noticed before when ploughing and working a field – an awareness of a vast, dark silence as if the soil has a presence as deep as an ocean.

30th

The crab apple seedlings I sowed back in January are starting to germinate, showing broad, green cotyledons and red stems.

31st

Spring is in the air! I went for a walk to look at the grazing for the cows and noticed that the plum trees in the paddock hedge are starting to come into blossom, there were insects about in the fields, some of them ladybirds. I noticed one of the ladybirds on a gorse flower, its red contrasting strongly with the yellow. Stitchwort is beginning to flower in the bottom of the hedges.

April

1st
A very sunny day. Went for a walk in the wood, it was amazing how light it was in amongst the bare trees – the ground flora was bathed in nourishing sunlight and making the most of it, when the canopy comes into leaf it will be gloomy in there.

2nd
Admired a cock pheasant on the other side of the paddock through binoculars. As well as the normal reds and browns he had a splash of blue like a jay on his wing feathers and his back.

3rd
I noticed today that the side of the drive is littered with last season's aspen leaves, looking like discarded tea bags. I picked one up and could see that the body of the leaf had been totally eaten away leaving only a delicate tracery of veins giving it the look of fine lace, so fine that when I held it over the palm of my hand I could see right through it and make out the colour and lines of the skin almost as clearly as looking through glass.

4th

Stepped out of the house just after sunset to go and look round and was surprised to see a bat silhouetted against the deep blue of the first darkening of the sky. Behind the bat, a star in the west shone over the Scots pine on the edge of the farmyard.

5th

Watched a wren flitting about by the pond. She would land on a small, thin branch lying out of the water and move from place to place on it apparently without any worry of falling into the water. Every so often a circle of ripples would appear where she had taken a quick peck at the surface. Of course her slight weight had no effect on the twiggy branch – it did not move at all under her.

6th

Ploughing a gently sloping field with a wood to the north west as the sun was setting which gave the illusion that as I went up the field the sun was moving horizontally amongst the trees.

7th

Found a complete bird's nest blown onto the floor of a shed by the wind - made of mosses, straw, twigs and finished with a delicate woven lining of cow hair!

8th

Sitting in the living room I saw a brown bird land with a flap in the weeping willow in front of the house. It was a female kestrel with some prey that I could not identify. She failed to keep her balance on the willow branch and had to descend to the lawn where she seemed to be waiting for the unfortunate victim to die, eventually starting to peck at it.

9th

There is a very distinctively coloured cock pheasant visiting the farmyard at the moment.

He is dark with shimmering green sides, purple and rust coloured shoulders and has red side panels on his head. He wanders around the yard apparently at home as a domestic foul, even announcing his presence with his proud call. I was surprised to find him within ten feet of the front of the parlour as I was milking this morning.

10th
White wild cherry blossom against a clear blue sky and the call of two wild geese as they fly over.

11th
There were a lot of cock pheasants around while I was ploughing today, at one point one was running along the bottom of the furrow in front of the tractor. Later on I was amused when another I had seen walking along one side of the field appeared on the opposite side quarter of an hour later – he must have walked all the way around the perimeter of the ploughing.

12th
I worked until well past dark last night to get the barley sown. After putting the tractor and seed drill away I walked back to the field to collect the landrover and trailer and saw an eerily beautiful sight.   The first stars had started to come out as I was still sowing and dark rain clouds built up from the west, but now a fan of silvery white light was refracted over the edge of the cloud bank.

The scale was tremendous, starting in the west passing overhead and reaching out of sight in the north east – a band of diffused light that seemed almost solid and something similar in the north at ninety degrees to the main band. I stood there for some minutes admiring it and had some idea of what it must be like to see the aurora borealis.   I cannot explain the source of light – the moon had not risen. A few minutes later it was gone leaving an ordinary night.

13th
The most notable creature at the moment is a woodpecker due to its regular loud drumming in one of the trees behind the yard. As I write this I can hear it from the house. It is a very distinctive sound, a resonant roadhammer. I wonder if he chooses a particular sort of tree for its sound qualities.

14th
Went in the copse at the side of the drive to get some cut branches for firewood. With the sun shining on the green grass and the flowering currant and wild cherry blossom and bees overhead it was like a natural, wild garden.

15th
Is there any bird more comical than the pied wagtail? I saw one this morning with a bunch of nesting material in its beak meandering across the yard in a

busy body sort of way, tail wagging up and down but not actually getting anywhere due to the constant changes of direction.

16th
As I was milking this morning I felt a sudden draft of fresh air on my forehead –
two robins had swooped into the parlour in the midst of their aerial battle and
turned around and left just as quickly.

17th
We were sitting in the living room this evening when the peace was shattered
by the sound of breaking glass. After a quick search of the house we found a
cock pheasant had flown through one of the second storey windows and was
sat there dazed but apparently unhurt. Each time I tried to let him out he
panicked and flapped up the unbroken side of the window so I had to reach
past him from a distance with a broom handle to open it.

18th
A grey drizzly morning so I was amazed to hear a bumble bee working the newly opened flowers of a willow tree as I opened a gate nearby.

19th
What an essential resource for bees and other insects early flowering fruit
trees must be. At the moment there are damson, wild black plums, pear and
wild cherry trees all in bloom. Together they must far outweigh the limited
ground flora flowers available in the garden and fields at this time, that will
soon change however as the fruit trees fade and the mass dandelion popula-
tion in our organic fields take over.

20th
Noticed a mining bee entering two or three tunnels in the short cut grass of
the lawn, the tunnels the exact size to allow her red abdomen to pass and a
tiny pile of excavated soil by each hole. I suppose she was placing the nectar
and pollen in each tunnel before laying her eggs, the resultant larvae will be
left with the food needed to grow and mature.

21st
A couple of seasons ago I was surprised to notice an old crab apple tree managing to survive below the cutting level of the top of one of the hedges – i.e.
growing within the hedge. It had a single blossom on it and I had hoped to

harvest the apple in order to grow progeny from it, but as I never found the fruit it is possible it failed to develop. I still keep an eye on it, hoping for a second chance to get some pips. When I checked it this evening I was struck by its form – the old, knarled trunk about five feet tall and ten inches wide, full of twists and whirls in the bark, the branching miniature canopy, restricted to the top line of the hedge but most of all the incredible silkiness of the newly emerged leaves when rubbed between finger and thumb.

22nd
How quickly wildlife can take advantage of some new habitat. This afternoon I noticed a bumblebee going underneath some black plastic I am using as a mulch along a newly planted hedge. I have also seen a robin perched on an apple tree I had planted only a few minutes before as I planted the next and a wren happily flitting from branch to branch on hawthorn plants planted the day before.

23rd
I think that the flora of Britain reaches its ultimate expression in deciduous woodland in spring. I went to our small wood to collect firewood today, but it was so pleasant in there that it was hard to concentrate on the task in hand. The warmth of the sunlight was caught by the shelter of the trees and the light seemed to have a different quality inside the wood. Wood anemone and celandine are flowering now and the leaves of bluebells and red campion are evident, promising the main show later in the season. The elderbushes are putting energy into their leaves and the sycamores are just beginning to open the first buds.

The wood is on a north facing slope and on damp ground so it can be cold but this also encourages moss growth which itself gives the place a special character. Timbers that were felled only two years ago are already completely carpeted with moss and I feel guilty about taking them for firewood – they are an excellent habitat for the creeping, crawling, secretive creatures. I always try to leave a pile here and there for them. One particular stack was covered in a continuous green velvet of moss and looked like a fine couch on which a faery queen might recline.

24th
I have just got to record this day. The weather was very kind - sunny and mild with a gentle breeze. There was a general feeling of ease and contentment

in the animals and the land itself. Summer had come early and the livin' was easy!

25th
The first shoots of barley are showing after a wait of two weeks. This is one of my favourite sights on the farm – rows of freshly germinated corn shining a phosphorescent green in the sunlight. It is pleasing to the eye to see how evenly they follow the contours of the field, vibrant confident growth - a sign of hope.

Noticed a cowslip growing on the front lawn, it has managed to flower since we last cut the grass.

26th
Watched an orange tipped bumblebee working the flowers of two blueberry bushes growing in pots in the little yard by the house. The flowers hold the promise of fruit to follow being already shaped like the berries and are big enough to allow the front half of the bee to disappear completely into them before re emerging to move onto the next flower. How multi-functioned these little bushes are – they provide food for the bee and us and allow us to avoid buying fruit in plastic trays flown from South America, if we can just wait for the season.

27th
I saw the first swallows today, first one and then in a few minutes six or seven more. It would be nice to think that they had literally just arrived.

28th
Noticed some cleavers or goose grass growing in the bottom of a hedge in a fenced off corner by the yard. The shade of the willow tree in the same enclosure has caused the rosettes of leaves to grow larger than normal, making it look like the "Umbrella Plant" houseplant.

29th
We have a robin around at the moment that I am sure is interacting with us humans. He comes in the milking parlour in the mornings to pinch flakes of cereal dropped by the cows, picking up a piece and then standing with head cocked to one side as if saying "I'm havin' this bit!" before flitting out. When I had the ladder up to the gable end of the house to clear ivy from the gutters he

appeared on the edge of the gutter looking down the ladder at me as if asking permission before hopping in to forage.

30th
When I went out of the house this evening to look around there were several bats flying around above the little yard in front of the house. Silhouetted against the darkening sky they flew as fast and as acrobatically as swallows.

May

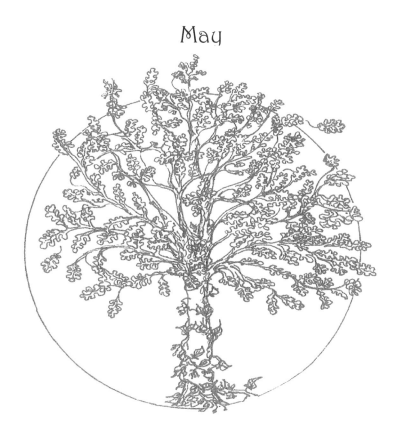

1st
It is impossible not to admire the way that things in nature fulfil their pattern and grow into their intended form. I have a Scots pine that I found growing in a gutter and transplanted into a tub. It is now two feet tall and this spring developed four shoots at the tip – I thought I would need to single them to one leader, but no – three of them have folded down to become branches leaving one to become the main shoot. Such graceful choreography.

2nd

When I checked the mole traps this evening I found a newt in the bottom of the mole run. I thought he was dead at first but he gradually came to life as I held him on the palm of my hand. Despite the distinctive black and orange colouring the most notable features were the blunt snout and the articulate digits of his feet. He held his tail curled to one side at first but gradually unfolded it. I would have loved to bring him home to the garden but decided to put him down in the rough grass under the hedge where I found him.

3rd

The yard is covered with drifts of beech blossom a couple of inches deep in some places. It has fallen from the beech trees, some standard green and some copper beech that grow on the east side of the house.

4th

An oak tree that I planted fifteen or twenty years ago has now grown to over sixteen feet tall and has a stem circumference of twenty inches at chest height. The main trunk has many branches that form the canopy and the fresh growth of this year's leaves filter and colour the sunlight forming a microclimate within the sphere of the top growth. A woody nightshade has scrambled up the stem and reaches seven to eight feet into the branches.

5th

The sun shining on a field of dandelion flowers scattered like a million stars in the night sky and sticking up in the middle – the tall red neck of a cock pheasant.

6th

Ah May! The birds are singing when we wake up at 5am and still singing when we go to bed. It is like an orchestra, there are the soloists who sing the main and most tuneful melody (the greatest of these, the virtuosos, are the larks), but even the lesser birds with plainer songs add their part, it might only be a chirrup of a few notes but it adds to the whole. The raucous call of the pheasant or crow punctuates the end of a movement and the symphony moves to the next. Distance adds to the variety, there are chattering swallows and cooing pigeons close to while the wilder birds add their contributions from afar, fading and fading out of earshot.

7th

Noticed the sun catching the newly emerged foliage of a favourite oak tree. It was as if the tree had burst into leaf in one morning.

8th

I was dismayed to find a nest of bumblebees inside a housing on one of the silage machines I prepared for work this morning. They were very docile and I was able to get them out one at a time and rehouse them in a pile of stones behind the yard. There was one large one followed by smaller, sleepier or half developed ones and finally some furry, sticky pods like small beans that were larvae I suppose.

9th

The cows are grazing a field called the Cwtsh yr Odin. There is something different about this field, it has the steepest slope on the farm – a bit hair raising on a tractor! There are more flowers in the hedgerows here then any other field – an almost continuous colony of dog violets are flowering now, very low in the turf below the bite of a cow, there is a good patch of primroses, there are harebells, bluebells and dog's mercury. All of these grow in other places on the farm but this is the only field were they all grow. I like to walk along the top hedge where the flowering gorse comes down to the grass and look out across the valley – this is possibly my favourite place on the farm.

10th

A balmy, idyllic day. About 5pm I got to the top of a field and noticed the crab apple tree was in flower, likewise the rows of wild cherry trees on either side of the drive – a tunnel of blossom that drops onto the drive like a thin dusting of snow and swirls up behind the car as we drive along.

11th

I was struck this morning by the variation in colours of the newly emerging tree leaves and what a perfect background the clear blue sky of a chilly May morning is for them. We have a row of mature beech trees behind the house, two of which are copper beech. Their dark purple contrasts with the fresh green of the usual beeches that surround them. The green of the apple trees is different again and that is different to the green of the pear trees. The biggest variation within a species is shown by oaks which vary from a bright yellow green through khaki, standard green to a brownish green. My favourite is the bright yellow green which is as pleasing as the lifting hues of an acer.

12th
The highlight of today was seeing a dragonfly. It had a yellow/gold body and startling wings – edged in black with a trellis work of black veins. The wing membrane itself was as clear as glass giving the impression of a delicate work of art in leaded glass.

13th
5.30am. The sky was clear blue and the sun only just above the eastern horizon. Its rays were shining horizontally through the new oak leaves and young cherry trees in blossom. This early in the morning and this low in the sky it gave a red tinge to the air making it almost tangible. Following the cows along the drive between the high hedges and trees I was out of sight of the curlew that flew warbling along the hedge before tipping up and over the drive against that eternal blue sky and continuing its plaintive calling. Perfect, just perfect.

14th
I wonder if the varying greens of all the emerging leaves in May truly are different and more special than the rest of the year or does it just seem that way to eyes that are hungry to see foliage after six months of winter? There are not enough green tinged words to describe the green of new beech leaves half unfolded, the green of new hawthorn leaves, of lime leaves, apple tree leaves, of delicate new larch needles and most importantly of all for the farmer – the relief of the sight of fields of sweet green grass and clover.

15th
Saw two bluetits fighting on the ground at the base of a hedge – a whirling ball of blue, feathery fury. They were so engrossed in their fight they took no notice of me for a few moments until finally breaking up and flying into the hedge at full speed.

16th
The afternoon that we rolled the seedbed after sowing spring barley a pair of lapwings appeared on the field. Now the corn has germinated they must be nesting in it as they are often to be seen wheeling around and piping their distinctive wild notes. I am always surprised at the wingspan of the bird in flight compared to its diminutive size on the ground with wings folded.

This morning I saw one of the pair in an aerial battle with a crow. To me just an interesting incident but for the bird a life or death situation as he or she battles with an intruder to save its offspring. When I passed again later there was a second crow waiting on the hedge. I sincerely hope the lapwings win through.

17th
Walked up through the wood along the boundary between an area of Scots pine planting and two full size oak trees - the area immediately below the canopy of the oaks was solid with bluebells, beneath the conifers only bare ground with occasional elder bushes.

18th
After heavy thundery rain last night this morning there is a tide line of yellow pollen on the yard wherever the puddles had been and in the field when we went for the cows a similar line of hawthorn blossom across the gateway.

19th
5am. The sky was clear and blue but a large bank of grey mist was moving northwards through the valley when we went for the cows. The main bank gradually dispersed but one area intensified becoming white and was situated in a specific area north of a farmyard across the valley where it seemed to coalesce into a hemisphere. When I looked back as I left the field it was completely gone.

20th
This evening as I walked up the drive and looked over the gate on the top corner I came more or less face to face with the slow, steady flapping of a heron in flight. The wingspan was the main impression, surely there is no other bird around here with that expanse of wing.

21st
After twenty years of interest in plants and of botanising around the farm I have found something I have always hoped for – orchids, Early Purple and only just on our land – a foot within our boundary on the extreme eastern margin of the farm. They look so exotic with their showy flowers and mottled stems. There is a colony of them on the local common about half a mile away, so perhaps the seed has blown in from there.

22nd
The partial cloud cover meant that Moel Fammau was in shadow but next to it Moel Fenlli was highlighted in sunshine. The high grass slopes were glowing

lime green while the heather clad hill fort above was darker green.

23rd
I have just been out to look at the cows – it's 8.15pm. The sun has finally come out after a fairly wet and grey day. The whole valley is flooded with golden light that illuminates the depths of the tree canopies. I am struck by the amount and volume of bird song, the air is filled in all directions with chirps, trills and tweets and on arrival back in the farmyard the contented chortling of the hens. It seems as if the whole world is content tonight.

24th
The skylarks seem very prominent this year. They dominate the sky when we fetch the cows in for morning milking. I do not remember noticing them like this last year. I am worried for their nests amongst the cow grass, hope they survive.

25th
Last night when cutting silage I disturbed a levret and then had to watch carefully to make sure I did not hit him with the mower. The next time I saw him two carrion crows were trying to catch him for tea. The little creature was only 7-8 inches tall but would make a run at the crows to drive them off and then try to escape but the crows would always return. How desperate the levret must have been to take on such determined hunters. I drove the crows off and he made for a corner of uncut grass left for grazing. I watched to ensure the crows did not return until he made it to cover. Perhaps I have interfered with the food chain and deprived the crows of a meal but they can always raid a garden for bread scraps as I have often seen them do, the levret deserved a break!

26th
 Following the first swath of silage on a field I came around a corner and saw a young fox sitting upright like a dog watching the tractor. He seemed reluctant to move, intrigued by the machinery. He did eventually slip into the hedge but was back again when I returned for the next load and then again a third time his inquisitiveness seemed to conquer his fear.

27th
Heard the cuckoo.

28th
A brood of wagtails must have just fledged when I went to see the calves this morning. The half feathered half downy chicks were making attempts at flight and landing on the calves' backs. Between the chirpings and crash landings and the puzzlement of the calves it was a scene of chaos.

29th
Saw two herons flapping in their ponderous way as they negotiated an electricity pole and its cables in our neighbour's field next to the village. Later I heard their raucous, gruff calls, perhaps alarming to Sunday morning sleepers in the houses nearby. Within a few minutes I could hear the calls of wild geese but could not see them. They burst into view over the canopy of an oak tree, five birds flying in V formation, full of the power of flight.

30th
Sitting in a favourite place on our recently cut lawn after breakfast I noticed that because of the heavy dew every single blade of grass (all the same height because of the mowing) had a bead of moisture shining in the sunshine. There must have been thousands if not millions of them, all identical.

31st
Surprised to see two honeybees working the inconspicuous flowers of a spindle tree at 8.30pm on a grey, damp evening. I suppose it was their last chance as it had been overcast and drizzly all day.

June

1st

Today I placed a tree shelter around a small oak I had noticed in a hedge while I was passing back and to carrying silage. It set me thinking about the sheer chance of things – whether or not I decide to protect that tree and let it grow up. Two minutes work now may make a big difference to the future – will there be no tree at that spot or will there be a fully grown hedgerow oak many years from now? Presumably the current hedgerow trees were chosen by country-folk one, two or three centuries ago and nurtured for the first few years, just enough to become obvious and therefore left by those who came next.

Whilst on the subject of hedgerow trees it occurs to me that the vast majority around here are oaks, especially if they stand alone in a hedge. There are a handful of ash and even less of any other species, and then only where there are many trees in a hedge as if the hedge was at one time neglected which allowed them to get a foothold rather than being deliberately chosen to grow on.

2nd

After a wet day following some sunny days there is a lot of moisture in the air. Looking round later than normal due to an evening out I saw the cows lying down in their field surrounded by a continuous circle of mist.

3rd

When we came out to get the cows in for milking this afternoon it was just starting to rain heavily, as I shut the gate by a small oak tree I noticed the last patch of dry concrete and when I got there the patter of rain drops on my waterproof coat stopped as I entered the rain shadow of the tree. Within a few minutes there was a deluge but it was warm enough to make it pleasant.

The same shower has battered the standing hay down, all facing the same direction in waves so that the field looks like a sea frozen in one moment. The few clumps of stronger grasses that have withstood the onslaught and remain upright look like the breakers.

4th

When we sowed the spring barley earlier this year the weather went very dry just after the corn germinated and the young plants sat there looking thin and starved. I was worried whether it would survive however the rains came and saved the crop which is now knee deep, lush green, strong and apparently invincible. As I picked docks out of it today I admired the strength of the spirit of the corn – how true the words of the folk song "John Barleycorn" which celebrates the death and resurrection of the corn, from sowing to harvest and resowing.

5th

Wagtails are so daft about where they will nest. We once had one build her nest on the back axle of a tractor, this year they have built in the open sided housing of the milk cooling compressor. I did not know until I heard the clamour of the chicks demanding food. The little mother is back and to feeding them and flies out to fend off the cows as they pass for milking. It must be a bit drafty in there when the compressor fan runs!

6th

As I was walking down our green lane the other side of the village I heard a chorus of chirps and saw a crowd of very small birds all moving as one group along one hedge and then crossing to the other. They were fledgling wrens, about eight or nine maybe more.

7th
Thundery showers are forecast for this afternoon and just after dinner it has gone very grey and breezy, threatening to rain. Then the sun came out making the big globular rain drops shine silver as they came hurtling down.

8th
Everything is food for something - I noticed a toadstool in the lawn about twice the size of a golfball, purplish brown with creamy coloured warts all over it. A lot of the surface had cavities eaten into it, revealing white flesh inside. Thinking about it, fungi are very often eaten in this way, even if poisonous to us some small creature can digest them safely.

9th
5.15am. The sun was shining very strongly through the cold, crisp air on to Moel Fammau. We could see every detail of the mountain, it seemed to be closer than normal and shining an intense green. There is a thrush that sings loudly and boldly on the top shoot of a cherry tree as we walk up the drive, he does not move even when I stop and speak to him.

10th
The larks were singing overhead as I lubricated the forage wagon in the yard. In the field a pair of pheasants spent the morning exploring the swathes of grass. Suddenly the cock pheasant flew across my path, when I looked to see why, a kestrel had landed on a swath. The pheasant must have been acting like small birds that mob a bird of prey.

We have harvested part of our hay field as silage this year to save work. There is a grass amongst the mixture of species in that old ley with a light purple flower that lies in the swathes looking like cut lavender, by the end of a day carrying silage the floor of the machine is covered in these heads looking like lavender pot pouri.

11th
5.30am. The wind moving every leaf of an oak tree into sound and the whole adding up to a roar. How often does that happen when no one is passing to hear it?

12th

We always rogue (pick by hand) the docks and ragwort out of the hay crop before we cut it, a job made bearable by the delight I take in the botanical diversity of the hay field – red clover, clumps of black medick, vetch, ribwort plantain (or fire grass as my grandad used to call it – because it is slow to dry out completely and might cause the hay to heat up due to being insufficiently dried), sorrel growing up to three feet high, buttercups and a variety of flowering grasses – timothy, meadow dog tail and false oat grass.

I read in the local paper recently that the age of a ley can be estimated by allowing seven years for every buttercup out of a sample of one hundred that has more than five petals. I tried it out this afternoon and found twelve with six or seven petals which equates to eighty four years since the field was ploughed. This fits in well with what I had been told.

13th

After thirty six hours of rain, heavy at times, there is water everywhere. There is a new stream running off one field under a stile and into the next field. I found a wren drowned in a water trough. The biggest surprise is a small patch of ground raised about six inches and squishy to walk on that bounces under the feet. There must be water trapped beneath the turf.

I saw a cinnabar moth on the path to the petrol station. The path runs through a patch of trees planted on what used to be the main road until it was rerouted when the town bypass was built.

14th

Moel Fammau looked very eerie this evening underneath a low layer of dark cloud with thick mist along the ridge in front of the mountain, leaving only the upper slopes and peak rising out of the slow flowing river of grey.

15th

Everywhere there are chicks in nests now. Swallows peer down at us from crowded nests in every building. There is a nest of blue tits in a hollow gate post in the yard that emit a constant urgent call for food. The hedges are alive with the sound of chicks that adds a dimension of vitality to them. Parent birds are back and to with mouthfuls of food, what work for them but it must also be the high point of their lives.

16th
What a harmonious, contented and worthwhile place an organic farm can be at its best.

The cattle are content and friendly, the pastures are in good heart, the corn grows well in unsprayed fields that allow a moderate amount of weeds as food for wildlife. The wildlife abounds because of the hedges and other habitats. If you can get the husbandry right then all is generous and productive with the same nourishing atmosphere as a well tended garden that cheers the hearts of visitors, neighbours and residents. This satisfaction is surely more important than mere units of production and the pure pursuit of profit.

17th
We have a length of hedge that is a continuous run of flowers at the moment – pink dog roses, white burnet roses, honeysuckle, briar flowers and elderflowers. The only sections that have no flowers are the short lengths where holly dominates in the shade of the oak trees. In the base of the hedge and out into the field are the annual and perennial plants – buttercup, wild parsley, groundnut, woundwort, bird'sfoot trefoil and a graceful thistle with flowers reminiscent of knapweed and stems less prickly and fleshier than creeping thistle.

18th
As we approach the summer solstice the sun is rising further to the north in the east and is fully above the horizon when we gather the cows at 5am. It throws my shadow a long way across the field, sometimes even as far as the hedge, making my darkling twin stand upright. The dew on the grass gives a shining corona to the edges of the giant image.

19th
I am always amazed by how small wrens are whenever I see them. As I went to check the cows this morning I noticed a wren hopping about on the track hardly bigger than the pebbles. Later in the afternoon a heron flapped its way over the farmyard – the largest bird we see here.

20th
I was working by a hedge that we cut back in the spring today and took the opportunity to see how it had grown back. It had been rather overgrown and that has led to an interesting regrowth. The upright stems that we cut are quite thick and have sprouted again at the top giving them the appearance

of forest trees in miniature. The hedge is completely clothed in this regrowth that looks like the forest canopy. Below this at floor level the flowers are flourishing due to the stimulus of extra light, in particular the dog violets. The cop rises up above the field just there and gives the whole miniature landscape the feeling of a wooded hillside.

21st

I found a hen partridge with ten chicks following her along the drive this morning, each of them no more than two inches in length with stripes of yellow and grey along their backs. The mother wanted to lead them into the long grass of the hedge but they seemed too small to cope with it. I wanted to pass with the tractor so had to wait for them to disappear. I went back later and thought they had gone and so set out only for them to pop out onto the concrete about halfway along, I had to follow them crawling along at the pace of the slowest chick. After many attempts to return to the hedge they eventually made it under a gate into the barley field.

22nd

There is something timeless about the long summer evenings. The sun is still high above the horizon at 9pm, its light gives a red/orange fringe to everything. It is as if this evening is outside of time, is simply a continuation of a calm, easy moment that has always been.

23rd

Found a moth when I was turning the compost in the garden. I picked him up and he clung to my thumb trembling in that way that moths do and then proceeded to wash one side of his head with a front leg and then the other side with the other leg. He seemed totally unconcerned about my presence. I placed him on the roughly fissured bark of an elder bush.

24th

As I worked in the doorway of the workshop this morning I noticed the smallest ladybird larvae I have ever seen crawling on my hand. It was not much more than a centimetre long and only two to three millimetres broad. After admiring it for a while I put it on a nettle leaf to hunt aphids. I always think that these larvae look so alien that maybe they should be killed on sight but of course far from being sinister insect invaders they are a useful predator in the garden.

25th

We baled and cleared the hay field yesterday, a very satisfying feeling when it goes well with plenty of sun and no rain. The field has not been ploughed in living memory and still has the ridges and riens of the old ploughing system. It has its own mixture of grasses different to the rest of the farm, a mixture that smells sweeter than the other fields. As the hay dries out the grass shrinks becoming a bluey green and the flowers dry out almost like pressed flowers, the buttercups keep their colour but the pink/red clover unfortunately turns brown. All in all it supplies the cattle with a pleasing mixture of species and a good mix of minerals. Also sun dried forage has higher levels of vitamin D important in calcium utilisation in a milk producing animal such as the cow. The crowning moment of the harvesting was seeing a scattering of dog rose petals on the side of a load like confetti where the trailer had brushed against the hedge on the way to the yard.

26th

Ten wood pigeons sitting in a row on the top rail of a gate.

27th

A sunny morning with some high cloud but I was intrigued by a long undulating ribbon of mist following the last ridge of higher ground in front of Moel Fammau. What atmospheric conditions lead to such phenomena I wonder?

28th

I always like to see yarrow flowering in the fields, it is such a cheering sight and reminds me of the family story of how my grandfather would pick a bunch of the pinker blooms to take to the house for my grandmother.

29th

Discovered a weasel drowned in a water trough, his body so slim and sleek. I was so sorry to find him lifeless, some animals are so secretive I only ever see them dead.

30th

This last week of June has been dominated by scent. The air has been heavy and muggy and fragranced with the sweet, light intoxicating aroma of white clover flowering in the fields and turning them white. On top of that are the dog rose and elderflower and the queen of them all – honeysuckle.

July

1st
I just noticed this in time to avoid stepping on it – a woven ball of cobweb strung between blades of grass attended by a spider. In the middle of the ball was a seething brown mass of minute but fully formed spiders.

2nd
It was a treat this morning to see the moorhens on the pond as I moved the electric fence for the cows. I heard some shrill calls as I approached that corner of the field and saw five of them on the water, some of them youngsters. The sound was similar to the alarm call of a blackbird. Eventually they saw me and all slipped away in different directions. By the time I finished moving the fence and walked back to the yard I could hear their calls again. It's not unusual to hear their raucous calls from the garden in summer, I think they must be an argumentative sort of bird.

3rd

Noticed a sprinkling of elderflower florets floating on the water in the cows' trough after an afternoon of wind. How pleasant for the cows – elderflower lemonade! Another trough had a potpourri of elderflower and rosehip petals.

4th

I don't know if mature oak trees are affected by a few weeks without real rain, surely they have deep roots but it was just starting to rain this evening as I passed a favourite oak and I wondered if that would be pleasant for it – the gentle drops, not quite a drizzle falling evenly all over its canopy. I hope it was pleasing to the tree and what a pure thing that would be, to be delighted in something as simple as rain – so much better than us humans with all our consumerist wants.

5th

It is very hot and muggy at the moment. Every time I go along our drive there are blackbirds sunning themselves on the concrete. This morning there were six in a row, all equally spaced from one another.

6th

5am. Close to rain when we went for the cows. Moel Fammau was highlighted against a bank of dark grey cloud. The low cloud overhead was causing the rising sun to cast a greenish gold tinge on everything. The mountain was shining brightly in this ethereal light, all browns and fawns. The clear air of the cold front made it appear much closer than normal and all the details of trees and folds of the slopes were picked out in detail.

7th

A Sunday evening, there is no wind, the sky is flat grey. There are no sounds from the village – no music or children playing, no youths shouting or football matches and for a moment no sound of traffic or airplanes. All I can hear is a ewe shouting for its lamb on a neighbouring farm, the twittering of swallows overhead and the meandering buzzing of a passing bee.

8th

Noticed a pair of juvenile moorhens on the pond. I had a good vantage point in the shade of the beech trees and downwind of them. How smoothly they move from swimming in the water to moving overland, gliding effortlessly out of the water and pacing about on their long articulated legs then back down to the water. They are greyish brown compared to the black of the adults. At one point one of them was preening his wings and fluffing out his tail in a shaft of late afternoon sunshine, all the time a strong breeze from the south kept up a constant flow of ripples over the pond surface giving it the appearance of a swift moving river.

9th
There has been quite a lot of wind this summer which has affected the trees more than winter wind because they are in leaf and more vulnerable to damage. In the dingle I was shocked to find a full sized oak tree snapped off half way up its trunk. The inner wood was not completely healthy but it was still a surprise to see this giant brought down. I also found about a third of the canopy of a small plum tree on the ground. I was sorry to see it as those plums are the first of the tree fruit each season.

10th
The sounds of a corn field – the murmur of the wind moving through the heads of barley, the twitter of swallows swooping after insects overhead.

11th
We started pulling the docks out of the wheat today, it is going to be a bit of a task as there are more than usual. The leaves of almost all the plants have been eaten to a latticework of veins as delicate as lace. The culprit is a shiny black/green beetle. Could this be a source of biological dock control? We couldn't be that lucky.

I have always thought that our unsprayed field of corn is a ten acre nature reserve rotated to a different location on the farm each year. It is sown in autumn and left alone until the following August providing a habitat for plants and animals. This year there is a more or less continuous understorey of wild pansies in places giving way to forget me nots, fumitory, mayweed and the occasional poppy.

12th
Saw a movement in the nettle patch when I went to get a sprig for nettle tea. I suspected a rat, but it was a full grown frog managing to balance on a leaning nettle stem.

13th

The air is fresh and clean after a week of off and on rain. The sky is blue and a pale half moon is riding high. The foliage of trees and bushes is clean and green and the scent of honeysuckle fills the air. I always smell honeysuckle before I see it and have to look around to locate the source of that idyllic perfume.

14th

I noticed a movement in the grazed stubble of the grass as I moved the electric fence, something was moving away from me but I could not make out what it was. Eventually I saw a vole moving up and down out of sight like a dolphin coursing through waves.

15th

After a day of constant rain yesterday there is some blue sky today. The Clwydian range looks magnificent in the morning sun – the ridge nearest here is in deep shadow thrown by a raincloud but beyond it Moel Fammau is shining in the sun.

I watched a hoverfly visiting a Welsh poppy in the garden, hovering with no apparent movement or sound of its wings vibrating, unlike the bumble bee that passed on its way to its nest in the rockery around the small pond.

16th

Waiting at the traffic lights in the village I saw a small bird with a moth in its beak fly out onto the road and hit it up and down on the tarmac, the moth fluttered and got free but the bird caught it again and flew back into the hedge.

17th

The oak tree that was felled by the wind back in January split into two halves as it fell and almost looks as if it was struck by lightning. The inside is almost hollow apart from the crumbly, reddish material that oak does eventually degrade to. The remaining upright stump is about three feet high and I noticed today that it has thrown out a couple of new shoots with fresh green leaves. When I clear away the rest of the tree for firewood I will leave the stump to regenerate so that it may grow into a wonderful knarled, hollow dwarf of an oak that might live on for a few more centuries.

The next tree is also half dead, three quarters of the crown has not come into leaf this year but in the peaty rotting tissue of a pruned branch there is a holly bush about two feet tall growing six feet above ground level.

18th

It is a great treat for me to be out and about in the fields early in the morning rather than stuck in the parlour milking. This morning was glorious at 5.30am, the sky was clear and the sun was shining strongly, promising a scorcher of a day and yet despite the obvious ascendancy of the sun and triumph of the coming day the romance and mystery of the night lingered on in the dewy grass and patches of mist hugging the lower ground. A fragile ring of mist surrounded the hillock at the bottom of the farm. All this magic reluctantly retreated as the sharply defined long shadows shortened with the sun's grow-ing strength.

19th

Four fledgling swallows sitting on an empty hay rack in the calf house, each one on a different level of the wire mesh like musical notes written on a stave.

20th

I disturbed a family of moorhens this morning as I took a tub of food to a newly calved cow in the field by the pond. The adults flew over an eight foot hedge to get back to the water, a juvenile followed on foot and last of all a furry looking chick scrabbled through the grass chirping in alarm. I have never seen moorhens fly before.

21st

We have had a bit of a heatwave over the last few days so it was a pleasant surprise to wake this morning and find it wet. There was a most gentle rain, a soft grey mantle touching everything as lovingly as a kiss to a child's bruise. There was only the slightest sound as the rain drops touched the broad leaves of a hazel when I tied the electric fence to the hedge. The world was closed in by various shades and shapes of the grey sky.

22nd

A very wet day. Across the valley, beneath the blanket of grey a bank of white cloud could be seen filling the quarry on the ridge between us and Moel Fam-mau.

In the yard, I saw a woodpigeon drinking from a puddle of water on an up-turned garage door.

23rd

A cabbage white butterfly (a "pest") perched with its wings folded on a blade of grass in the rain. Veined marble wings and a line of tiny, delicate rain drops along its antennae.

24th

Very heavy rain showers this afternoon. I put a three gallon bucket underneath the downspout of the biggest shed and it filled in ten seconds! When we went for the cows later on the rain had stopped and the sun had come out, we looked back along the track and there were dozens of green veined butterflies fluttering here and there in the lee of the hedge. How does something so delicate survive such downpours?

Tonight when I walked back from shutting the cows in after milking the same butterflies were feeding on brambleflowers in the evening sunshine. When stationary with their wings open they looked like extra flowers on the hedge, occasionally they would rise in small groups and resettle – as if the flowers were rearranging themselves.

One of the foodplants of the green veined white is charlock which is a terrible weed for us in the growing corn so at least there is a positive side – if we sprayed the crop there would be no charlock and therefore no clouds of green veined whites.

25th

8.45pm. The light is very eerie – a greenish gold. The sun is almost setting in the north west and the last rays are shining horizontally across the land below a low ceiling of grey cloud that intensifies the effect. Everything is gilded with a warm, otherworldly glow. Five minutes later the sun sinks a little lower and the moment is gone.

26th

I noticed a length of holly in the hedge with new shoots of growth, two to three inches long and lime green, much lighter coloured than the mature leaves. Although shaped like the older leaves these young leaves are not prickly being completely soft to the touch. The green of the leaves is the same colour as the unripe berries that cluster along the stems of the older growth.

27th
Leaning on the gate looking at the barley I noticed streams of heads of grain moving in scurries of light breeze that I could not hear or feel, intangible air currents only revealed by the corn.

28th
This morning Moel Fammau was shining green in the early morning sunshine but as the day clouded over by mid morning it looked like a black and white photograph – the light grey of the mountain contrasting with the dark grey to black of the closer ridges. This evening when I looked round the summit was lost in banks and folds of grey cloud that look like marbled steel.

29th
Noticed the dried out seed heads of the garden bluebells that have naturalised around the pond sat on top of their stems like pennants on flag poles.

30th
The ridge of hills across the valley was lost behind a curtain of rain that I could see advancing as I went for the cows this evening. The wind was blowing the undersides of the aspen leaves up, everything seemed grey and almost wintery. The shower arrived and passed over and the hills reappeared quickly.

Noticed groups of fifteen to twenty green veined white butterflies gathering in hoofprints and hollows in the mud of a gateway. I don't know if they were after water or getting something else from the mud.

31st
5am. The upper hills across the valley were covered in cloud but the lower ridge, directly opposite us was clear and one small square was illuminated by a ray of sunshine managing to get through the grey skies, that small patch of slope was golden green, hedges and trees glowing, and grew more so as I watched. Later on the weather closed in and it was very wet for the rest of the day.

August

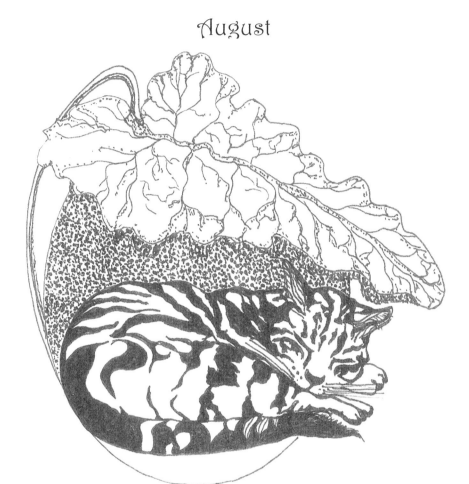

1st

As I was collecting silage this afternoon I came around a corner of the field to find two buzzards investigating the ground uncovered when I lifted the previous swath. I am always surprised by their size close up, I noticed particularly their thick looking legs, made so by the feathers I suppose. On the next time round they had been joined by a third companion.

2nd

It's amazing how quickly a sense of sylvan atmosphere establishes itself in a new plantation. When the town's bypass was built less than twenty years ago a new roundabout was built about fifteen yards away from our roadside hedge, the redundant road was grubbed up and the area restored and planted with trees. With the change in ownership the original hedge has not been cut and the hazel has grown up into mature bushes that lean out over the path towards the planted oak, ash, rowan and sycamore trees. Aspen has suckered out from the hedge and is shooting up in the mown verge beyond the new trees. The effect is of a woodland ride with yarrow, knapweed and red clover flowers visited by butterflies and other insects. All this on an area that was previously a main road.

3rd
Found a wasp nest that had been dug out by a badger. About ten wasps re-mained, moving around the papery remnants of their papery palace. I don't know if they were attempting repairs or salvaging food but when one flew out towards me I made myself scarce, not wanting to be held responsible for the damage!

4th
What a good saying "in clover" is, the sight and smell of a field of clover in flower is very heartening – acres of innumerable white flowers with bees hap-pily (if not drunkenly) going from blossom to blossom instil a feeling of wellbe-ing in the beholder.

We got caught in a thundery downpour when we went to get the cows in this evening. We could see a curtain of swirling rain approaching, falling more like silver snow than rain. When it reached us the drops were big and globular and it was easy to imagine them bouncing and wobbling if you caught them on the palm of the hand. There was little time to enjoy the sight though as we had to retreat rapidly to avoid a soaking.

5th
The robins are looking tatty now, their red breasts are dulled to a reddish brown. They look grey and drab and stand around watching us like old men. A summer of breeding and fighting has brought them to this.

6th
As I went to see the cows this evening the sun was setting over Rhes Y Cae mountain throwing off a fierce red glow. What caught my attention was the barley, which is actually a deep gold at the moment but in that light of the sunset it had took on a red glow. This set me thinking about how much more than straw and grain a crop of corn can yield. There is an aesthetic crop too –

the miracle of germination over an entire field and the stubbly green mantle thickening every day, the pleasure of an even, clean crop of corn ripening. In a breeze, ripples travel across the field in ever varying patterns, this can be disconcerting if you are standing in the corn, you almost feel that you will be swept of your feet.

7th
Despite having to abandon silage making for today because of rain I just had to admire the grandeur of the shower that actually stopped us. I could see it moving down the valley towards us, a vast dark cloud hugging the ground and obscuring everything on the far slopes as it travelled, leaving the church tower silhouetted against a wall of lighter grey behind. I thought it would pass us by at first but soon we were enveloped on all sides by a curtain of heavy rain that overwhelmed the grids in the yard causing puddles on which floated wisps of silage dropped off the machinery. Having bowed to the inevitable and decided not to go back to the field for another load I could not even leave the tractor because of the rain.

8th
Looking round in the dusk on a wet evening I saw a ghostly looking moth on the red brick wall of an outbuilding. It was creamy white with two curving fawn coloured thin stripes across its wings.

9th
The buzzards are very prominent just lately. There was one perched on a gatepost as I drove along the drive today. Earlier I had seen a crow mobbing one above a field of silage we were clearing, when I returned for another load twenty minutes later the altercation was still going on.

10th
Walked into the garden just as a half eaten apple core dropped out of the Bramley apple tree. I looked up to see what the culprit was but could see nothing – I suppose it was a grey squirrel.

11th
Cut our newest reseeded ley for silage. It has developed a delightful community of flowers this summer – corn poppy, corn marigold, white clover, red clover and....lentils – because I had put some old seed sprouting packets of seed in the mix. It was interesting to see their pink to white flowers on tall stems and

the fat seed pods with small green lentils inside. Adding to the colour were a hen and two cock pheasants with their colourful heads who dodged the mower for most of the cutting but finally gave up and slipped away as the last of the grass fell.

12th

5.30am A small patch of red sky where the sun was rising grew until all the eastern sky was streaked red. A delicate curtain of rain was shot red and in the west a red tinged rainbow appeared and then a second. This turned out to be a spectacular case of "red sky in the morning – shepherd's warning" as it was very wet later on.

13th

The cows are grazing the regrowth on our hayfield, the eighty year old ley with a unique mixture of grasses that always smells so nice when cut. When we collected the cows this morning the same aroma filled the air after a night of being walked on and cropped off by the cows, it was as aromatic as walking on a chamomile lawn. The cows were very happy lying in the early morning sunshine – I wonder will they recognise the sweet aroma of these grasses when they eat the hay bales in the winter and be reminded of their summer idyll?

14th

About eighteen months ago when cutting the hedge around the paddock I left a hazel bush to grow on in order to produce hazelnuts. This year the bush is bearing nuts and so far seems to have escaped the attentions of the grey squirrels. To try to beat the squirrels I am starting to use the nuts before they are fully ripe. How I enjoy the triads of nuts sheathed in their jackets that look like the crowns of playing card kings and the delicate rose bloom on the nut shell as it moves towards ripeness.

15th

Saw a group of eight lapwings on the rough grazing land this morning. I hope it is the pair that nested in the spring barley with their brood but they might be "strangers" forced in by the mighty breeze that has been blowing today.

16th

Stopped to admire the flowers on a burdock plant growing by the woodpile and counted over two hundred, similar to thistle flowers and turning darker purple as they mature before finally drying to the brown burrs that stick so well to the hair of dogs.

17th
A robin was singing on the collecting yard this morning as I was milking, his song a delightful free form improvisation above the strict pulsation of the parlour.

18th
It was darker than normal this morning due to the overcast sky and the mist condensing on the hedges and pasture. As I moved the fence I felt the first gentle drop of rain, so delicate that I was not sure it was rain and then a moment later another. The drops seemed to be the last essence of night quietly forming and falling to earth from the lightening sky. The general atmosphere was so pleasant that it did not matter that this was the beginning of a wet day. By the time I got back to the yard the concrete was wet and the rain fell in earnest while I milked but I had the honour of witnessing the first drop.

19th
We have had quite a lot of thundery rain this week. It began on Wednesday night with a real downpour. I had cleared a gutter on the house but could see from an upstairs window that the top of the downspout was blocked so the morning after the deluge I went up again and cleared it. When the rains came again last night the flow had been corrected and the water issued safely from the bottom of the downspout. It is pleasant to think of the path of the water, off the roofs and into the gutters, down and across the yard to the grids and along the dark unknown paths of the old drains below the fields dug in generations ago to emerge in the stream in the dingle. The stream leaves our land and travels about a quarter of a mile to the river Alun which joins the Dee and then on to the mother of the rain - the sea.

Thunder rain is reputed to be especially beneficial for plants if only because it contains more nitrogen than ordinary water so I always try to fill the watering cans for the greenhouses after a thunder shower. Thunder and lightning also remind us of the power of nature, harvesting plans have to wait, the TV and radio are off because we take the plugs out to protect the equipment. The only thing to do is stand and watch the drops bouncing off the yard, the sheet of water moving across the concrete and the flash flood puddles building up as the grids fail to cope.

20th
Cloudy and windy with showers. I noticed a broad band of sunlight breaking through the greyness and striking the other side of the valley, gradually advancing down the slopes. Curtains of drizzle filled the ribbon like shaft, looking almost like smoke.

21st
It seems to be a good year for crab apples, the trees are crowded with fruit – I counted fourteen apples on a twelve inch length of branch on one tree. Although the crab shows what human ingenuity has done with plant breeding – we have produced fruit three or four times bigger than the original and so much sweeter, it is still a generous plant, taking water and nutrients from the soil and combining them with sunlight to produce food, locking up carbon and producing oxygen into the bargain. The sight of apple trees bearing fruit gives such a feeling of wellbeing, it is truly a paradisical fruit.

22nd
As I was cutting a field of silage this afternoon I noticed a hen pheasant standing as tall as she could. I realised that she must have a nest or chicks there so I stopped, not wanting to kill them with the mower. The mother flew off as I approached so I found the chicks who could flutter a few feet only and then burrow amongst the grass making it impossible to find them all. I found one and placed him in the corner of the field and went back to mowing hoping that the others would have slipped away. Straight away the hen was back – what bravery! I left that part of the field and went to work at the other end to give her a chance to lead the chicks to the safety of the hedge which she did eventually.

23rd
Noticed one of the cats sleeping in the shade of a single burdock leaf that was broad enough to completely shade her like a parasol.

24th
5.30am. The moon was gilding the edge of a cloud with silvery white light and then rose above the cloud and across a patch of clear sky, disappearing behind the next bank of cloud.

8.30pm. After a day of sunshine and heavy showers I went to look round and it was still bright half light but the bats were out, the earliest I have ever seen them out, giving me the opportunity to see them better - how they flit and zigzag in all directions. Because of the light and the restricted feeding opportunities in the day due to the weather the swallows were still flying – and so the day shift and the night shift were out at the same time.

Further along the drive, silhouetted against the now darkening blue sky of dusk a big heavy bumble bee winged drunkenly past, returning from the last flight of the day.

25th
An autumnal breeze was blowing, threatening rain. At the bottom of a sloping field a group of swallows were swooping and then remaining almost stationary beating their wings like humming birds.

26th
As I walked up the drive this morning a southerly breeze was blowing leaves off the cherry trees on one side and carrying them horizontally across the drive into the trees on the other side.

27th
As I bent down to pull a ragwort I noticed a grasshopper jump from it as if abandoning ship. The first jump was about ten inches high, the next was two feet and then another of eight inches. That biggest jump would be equivalent to a human jumping a hundred feet high!

28th
I have been combining our field of barley this week and the major feature of the work has been the continuous presence of the buzzards. Every time I was stopped with some problem they could be heard and seen wheeling overhead. I began to feel that they had their eyes on me! The work was going so slowly they could well have thought that here was something on its last legs.

That field is on the other side of the road to the main farm and the buzzards seem more prominent there than on our side. My neighbour tells me that he has seen six together and thinks that they have a nest in the trees on the grounds of an adjoining house. Their call is so eerie, they seem as if they are never content but must always be out on the wing calling out their sadness at some condition unknown to us – perhaps a doom laid on their race for some sin in the past?

29th
Twenty or thirty swallows were swooping and soaring around the front of the combine as I worked this evening, oblivious to the danger of the machine and only occasionally having to swerve to avoid each other. A pair of buzzards circled and landed on the swaths looking for prey. The final sight of them was of one of them silhouetted against the dusk sky carrying something in its talons back to the nest.

30th
There is a small area at the side of the drive that I have protected from the cows because of a pile of gravel stored there (they love to play in things like that, bulldozing the pile with their heads). This has allowed it to grow up in weeds but it almost looks like a colourful garden. There is a seven foot mullein plant (native but an escape from our garden in this case), masses of rosebay willowherb, some in flower and some run to seed with their two to three inch long red seedpods that are as colourful as the flowers, the purplish red flowers of thistles, the broad foliage of coltsfoot, the spires of marestail and the spreading ground elder. Earlier in the year there was a carpet of yellow coltsfoot flowers followed by cowslips.

31st
Sunlight filtered through a canopy of oak leaves highlights a clump of dog violets in the bottom of the hedge. Tightly clustered together, younger lighter green leaves push up through the darker mature leaves. The whole clump is over a foot in diameter.

September

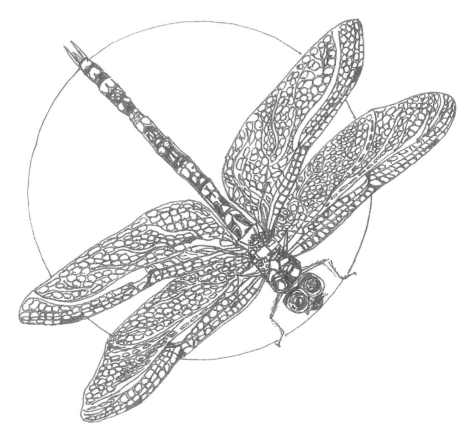

1st

Each year I wonder anew at the ability of the combine to separate grain from the chaff and straw. Very often I find the empty shells of chaff still attached to the straw in the swath looking like an entire head of wheat but completely empty. The grains are all safely in the grain tank sieved and separated even from the bigger weed seeds by the combination of draught and sieves inside the machine.

I was amused to walk around the corner of a shed today and find a fat wood pigeon pecking stray grains from the floor of a bale trailer that we had emptied only hours earlier. Life must seem so easy to him now, with food everywhere on the stubble fields, on the farm track, in the farm yard and a content non threatening farmer!

We have now cleared all the grain and straw from the corn field. After worrying about pigeons, sparrows and crows raiding the corn as it ripened it is pleasing now to see all the birdlife descending on the stubble to feast on the spilt grains. It is the numbers that impress – there is a flock of about a hundred crows. They are an impressive sight, either on the ground, each keeping a jealous eye on his neighbour or wheeling around on the wing in a large quarrelsome cloud. Amusingly, there has also been a tame racing pigeon walking amongst the stubble pecking here and there at grains. He is ignored by the wild birds as if not worthy of their attention. Somewhere a fancier is cursing him for not returning home from a race.

2nd
A wonderful halflight when we went for the cows at 5am this morning, not from the dawn but from moonlight. It struck me that part of the attraction was that rather than the near horizontal source of the dawn this light was falling gently from above, floating down through the early morning cloud and dusk like noon sunlight through a shallow sea to the sea bed.

3rd
There was a buzzard perched on a large clod on the ploughed land when I arrived to continue ploughing. After a while he half extended his wings in a gesture of "let us prey". Later on I noticed a mouse running along the cut furrow. It hid under a clod where the tractor wheel would pass so I stopped to move it and as I bent down to pick it up I saw it curl itself around its hairless, pink baby, even that size of life form has an impressive maternal instinct. I moved them both onto the ploughed ground. There is an old saying "Let not the plough stand idle to kill a mouse" - hopefully stopping work to save one is more acceptable!

4th
I think that butterflies epitomise autumn as much as falling leaves. They seem more prominent now, supping on fermenting fallen apples and late flowers such as the ice plant. Today I climbed over a fence by an oak tree that has a swollen bole at ground level making a handy step. As I put my foot down I disturbed a group of seven or nine tortoiseshells, impossible to count because of their flying pattern – rising, falling, disappearing behind the tree but always returning to the roughly fissured bark where they would land and flicker from sight as they folded their wings and by all appearances became a flake of old bark by presenting the camouflaged undersides of the wings.

5th
There is a crab apple tree in the back corner of the field that we are ploughing at the moment. It is festooned with small apples, some all green, some half green and half red and some all red but all weighing down the branches.

6th
I could see out across a solid bank of cloud that filled the valley this morning as I brought the cows in for milking, as tall as County Hall (a five storey building). Street lights half way up the opposite side of the valley were gilding the edge of the undulating surface. The effect was of new land extending to the other side.

Combining in difficult conditions because of frequent autumnal lows sweeping across the country. About 8pm this evening I was dismayed to see it drizzling on the windscreen of the combine tractor but it went off quickly and when I reached the bottom of the field and looked back up the slope I was pleased to see a full moon, the harvest moon rising between clouds in the east.

7th
I have had a busy couple of weeks and being working until 9pm the last two nights so getting up to milk at 5 am has been tough, but it was such a pleasant morning today that it was a pleasure to be out so early. It was dark but there was a warm but blustery wind. In the gloom the landscape seemed epic in proportion, our plantation of young trees towered over me as I collected the cows and I felt dwarfed by the elements. The field was by the road so the amber road lights cast a warm glow over me and the cows. It all seemed magical, Tolkienesque even.

8th
I saw a yellow frog with black speckles when I moved the fence this morning.

As I drove back along the farm drive in the tractor this afternoon I was "buzzed" by a double winged dragonfly that appeared over the hedge swooping back and to looking like a WW1 bi-plane.

9th
After a very wet night the clover leaves in one of the fields are covered with silvery drops of water. The older leaves have the best cover as if their surface allows the best surface tension in the drops. Because clover tends to grow in

patches it looked like areas of diamonds amongst the grass.

10th
Noticed a feather hanging on a single strand of cobweb circling this way and that and catching the rays of the sun.

11th
I realised today from the quiet and empty sky above the farmyard that the swallows have left. The last time I noticed them particularly was two days ago when I was milking.   There was a great number of them all spaced equally along the roof ridge of one of the buildings.   Each one was preening itself, some lifting a wing at one angle to the left or right, some turning their heads left or right and some lifting both wings – they looked for all the world like a line of semaphore characters!

12th
There are a lot of daddy long legs in the field that the cows are grazing at the moment. Groups of a dozen or more rise just in front of my feet, flying about two feet away and then landing again only to be disturbed when my stride reaches their new position.   They look like Victorian fairies moving from stem to stem.

13th
Noticed a faded yellowy green rose leaf on the lawn that had pulled into a ladle shape as it wilted, holding a tablespoonful of clear bright water after the rain.

14th
I wonder what mechanism allows mountains to apparently attract mist and cloud about themselves? After a damp night the sun was shining this morning and Moel Fammau was clear but Moel Fenlli was wreathed in white, woolly cloud that eventually moved into an impersonation of its flat summit. Ten minutes later Moel Fammau was also covered with a rolling shroud of grey.

15th
The cow track has many inch high clover seedlings growing on it, especially where the rain has washed silt into miniature mud flats. This is the result of the cows grazing clover that has flowered and gone to seed. The seeds pass through the cow and are deposited randomly around the farm, there are even some seedlings growing in the concrete joints around the dairy door.

16th

Came out of the house to find the weather very humid, grey and blustery. Suddenly there was two big flashes and then a crack of thunder – a lightning storm at 7.30 in the morning! Later I had to shelter under a large oak tree whose massive half dome shaped canopy has a diameter of seventeen yards. It was pleasant enough in the green shade with a persistent heavy drizzle out in the open and a regular fall of bigger drops from the circumference of the canopy – like being under the carousel of a merry go round.

17th

I was amused to find four harvestmen squat down together on the upperside of a nettle leaf. When they realised I was there they all lifted up on their articulated legs and walked over the side of the leaf together in one mass.

18th

When I moved the electric fence this evening I came across a hare on its form. It did not move even when I talked to it so I bent down to stroke it but as soon as my fingers touched its back it bolted off at full speed.

19th

After a sunny afternoon it clouded over and rained when I went to shut the cows in. Across the valley, underneath the grey sky banks of steam or cloud were rising from Moel Fammau and glowing white against the grey as the sunlight caught them.

20th

The lane up to the yard is covered in acorns and fir tree seeds after a windy afternoon yesterday. The acorns vary in colour from bright green to brown, the brown ones look seasoned and crunch underfoot, surely they have not managed to stay on the tree since last year? It surprises me that pheasants and pigeons can eat acorns considering that they cannot chew them before swallowing but must take them down whole and grind them up in the gizzard. This evening I walked down the lane and disturbed a group of five partridges amongst the acorns and they are even smaller birds. They must be eager for something there because when I looked again five minutes later they were all back again.

I could not identify the fir tree seeds at first but I think they are from the Grand fir that share the wind break around the yard with Douglas fir and Scots pine.

They lie on the yard like little brown plaques of bark and smell highly resinous when picked up, shaped something like the two lobes of a Gingko leaf each half has a seed embedded in the woody flake. The smell is very strong, as strong as pine disinfectant and takes me back to boyhood when I used to climb a tree behind the yard. The bark had occasional blisters full of the sap that could be popped with the fingers to release the powerful scent although the fingers then remained sticky and grubby for the rest of the day!

21st
As I walked down the drive hill tonight to shut the cows in the sun was shining through the wood across the drive and illuminating the big sycamore on the other side, giving it a greenish gold hue. All the rest of the hedge was in shade, only the tree trunk shone with this light.

22nd
We have had a spell of extraordinary weather over the last two weeks – dry and sunny, very kind weather. To illustrate the point – it is the first time all summer that we have emptied the rainbarrels by watering the greenhouses.

This morning was very pleasant when we brought the cows in for milking at 5am. Although still dark there was enough cloud cover to reflect a gentle yellowish light from the street lights. The air was mild and all was quiet. It is strange how minute variations make every day, every moment even, unique. A street light further down the valley was very prominent because it cast a funnel of light up through the tree tops that surrounded it, looking like a turret of light set in the woodland canopy. Another light far across the valley, perhaps ten miles away seemed to be shining intensely.

23rd
Discovered a small hawk in the slurry pit, trapped on the last uncovered piece of concrete floor. She was unable to fly – either a fledgling or because her wings and tail were wet with slurry. I caught her and washed the feathers – a task complicated by her fierce grip on my gloved fingers. About half way through the process she started making a piercing, keening cry – very unsettling. In order to release her I had to take the glove off and leave them both on the paddock grass. She flopped off, still uttering her eerie wail. I hope she makes it.

24th

It was threatening rain as the sun set this evening – rolls of misty cloud were moving along the ridge of Moel Fammau and to the north west a bank of white rain cloud was illuminated vivid orange by the sun which was sinking below the hills.

25th

After a shower of rain while I was ploughing a rainbow appeared at the other end of the field, looking like a continuation of the furrows.

26th

A very wet silvery dew on the grass this morning. I left a dark trail as I walked over the fields. I realised I could have created symbols and "crop circles" by walking in the desired shape if I had wanted but all my art would have faded away as the sun dried out the grass.

27th

Saved a very bedraggled bumble bee from drowning in a water trough. He was clinging to a bit of leaf as a life raft. I picked him out and balanced him on the hedge where he slowly straightened one leg and then another, gradually recovering as he dried out.

28th

Watched a pair of bats flitting about, silhouetted against a blue sky fading to red over the Clwydian range and the large crescent of the new moon set low in the sky above Moel Fenlli.

29th

Saw a squirrel running along the top rail of the garden fence carrying a pear pil-fered from the paddock in front of the house. Amusingly the pear was upside down – the blunt end in his mouth and the stalk pointing down.

30th

It is surprising how many cars are on the road at 5.30am on a Sunday morning. On a still morning like today there is a car to be heard almost continuously on one or other of the roads within earshot.

The dual carriageway past the farm entrance is lit with street lights that cast their gentle amber light a considerable distance onto the fields, the grass is lit even fifty yards away from the road and as I untie the gate my shadow is cast onto the dewy, orange illuminated pasture. The light also falls through the leaves of the trees in the wood, filtered and manipulated until it arrives at the wood floor where it touches the tussocks of wild grasses and woodland plants. Above all this, this morning the half moon was close to Orion and a faint corona surrounded them both.

There are many subtleties and plays of light that can only be seen at night as they are obscured in daylight. A light on the community centre in the village hundreds of yards away from the farmhouse throws the silhouette of tree branches onto our landing wall and yet all is darkness between us and the village.

October

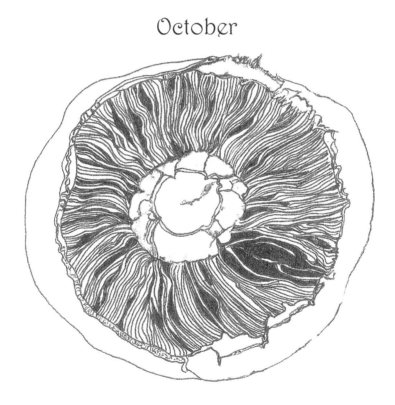

1st
There is a gale force wind tonight and heavy rain is forecast but it is pleasant to be outside. The high broken cloud is being blown across the full moon in

varying layers, each layer moving at a different speed. The silhouettes of the trees have sharp edges but are blowing wildly in the breeze. The whole effect is like an old sepia or monochrome photograph.

2nd
Noticed an acorn suspended by a thread of cobweb from an oak branch, hung by its main stem with a secondary tail with minute undeveloped acorns it appeared to be floating like a fairy helicopter designed for them by Leonardo da Vinci.

3rd
The moon light is very bright tonight, casting a shadow from one of the oak trees that is four or five times the size of the actual canopy.

4th
5am. Everything was enveloped in slight, low lying cloud that felt like the lightest possible drizzle on the skin, it reflected any source of light making it relatively light for that time in the morning but the light seemed to play tricks – the tall chimney at County Hall looked like a monument – Cleopatra's needle or similar, the three roof peaks of a house in the town looked like a gothic mansion where there is none.

5th
Noticed five magpies standing around a hawk on his catch – a woodpigeon, they seemed to be trying to bully him in order to steal the carcass but he faced them down and they left, leaving him to his prize.

6th
It is very windy but pleasant outside tonight. The full moon is illuminating the clouds in such a way as to make them look of more substance than they are, as solid as the canopies of the oak trees that catch the moonlight in differing ways. Some of them are simply silhouetted darkly against the sky and throw the light around their edges while others seem to let it deep into the canopy and seem to gleam silver.

7th
Today I saw the first puffball of the season, sitting there amongst the first scattering of brown oak leaves on the tufted autumn grass. A perfect, pure, fresh white globe as big as a football, unconcerned what man or beast might think

of it, intent on its own workings, on completing its mysterious life cycle. This visible orb is the culmination of its dark secret life below ground, a reminder of the rich but unseen processes of the soil beneath our feet. It is said that there is more livestock in the soil than walking around on top of it!

It strikes me now that autumn is the season for this dark secretive magic – the fungi that breakdown the remains of other lives, the ripening of fruit on the hedgerows, the fermenting and rotting of fallen fruit.

8th

We saw an incredible sight this morning when we went to the field to get the cows in for milking. The air was completely still and beneath the stars and faint light of the waning moon undulating layers of fog had formed, so that it seemed as if the air had solidified and we were walking into an oil landscape painting. Our normal landscape of trees and hedges had been replaced by an ethereal moorland of light and shade.

9th

The weather has been kind for over a month now, dry and sunny. Today I sowed the winter wheat in perfect conditions, the soil was dry and crumbly, hazy sunlight and a cold but gentle breeze from the south east that was just enough to bring down the occasional leaf from the oak tree in the middle of the field. I was struck by the sunlight on the brown leaves and the fat shiny acorns lying on the furrows around the tree.

The usual crows and seagulls that accompany any working of the soil were joined by five peewits strutting around and flying away a few yards whenever the tractor got too close. Their plumage had a greenish sheen, a detail that it is possible to see from the tractor as creatures are less wary of machinery than a human on foot.

10th

Looking out of the kitchen window this morning I noticed a nuthatch investigating the pots and planters we have in the front yard, finally finding what looked like a beech nut in the corner by the window he then hopped up onto a planted up old concrete water trough and found somewhere to hide his treasure in the fissures of the concrete. He returned to foraging in and out of the pots but quickly moved on elsewhere.

11th
How magical the world of the tree canopy dwellers (squirrels and birds) must be in autumn when the leaves turn. Their world must be flooded with light and colour as the dense green transmutes itself into golds, yellows and browns – a burst of radiance before the greyness of winter sets in.

12th
It occurred to me tonight that the first frost is one of the most definitive nights of the year. Gradually the nights get colder, then perhaps back off again becoming milder, one night it will be very clear at bedtime and yet cloud over before morning preventing a frost. Sometimes the coldness is due more to dampness and only appears to threaten frost. Then finally one morning the grass is covered in hoar frost that collects on the wellies as you walk through it. Here this may happen down the fields in hollows and where the land slopes away to the lowest point of the farm. I do not count those nights, for me the first frost is counted on the night it appears in the farmyard and (this is the real benchmark) destroys the leaves of the tender plants in the garden – most dramatically the nasturtiums, which collapse and hang down as if they had melted. There is no such marker at the other end of the year for although we may tell ourselves that there will not be another frost from late May there is always that chance and we will wake to find the foliage of our carefully tended early potatoes blackened. But once the first frost has arrived, although there may be further mild spells we know that the wheel of the year has turned and that summer is no more.

13th
As it turned out today was the first frost and I heard it before I saw it! – I could hear the grass crunching underneath my wellies in the dark when we collected the cows for milking.

14th
Watched midges of some sort dancing in a shaft of autumn sunlight. They would rise about eight inches and then drop to their original position again sometimes in pairs but singly too, sometimes joining together in groups of four or five and then ascending a foot or more.

15th
A wonderful clear morning, Orion and the other constellations bright in the dark overhead when we went for the cows. In the predawn gloom a bank of

mist was rolling up and over a hedge by the yard. Later the dawn came – clear blue sky and the sun making banks of mist shine gold and white with long shadows from the trees cutting through.

16th
I noticed a colony of tiny toadstools, barely two inches tall and a third of an inch in cap diameter growing in the turf beneath an oak tree. They covered a huge area relative to their size so that they formed a miniature heathland interspersed with growing "trees".

17th
Went for a walk to inspect a hedge along the top of the bypass embankment to see how it could be laid. This involved squeezing past a traffic barrier to get onto the embankment and once through it was like stepping into a different world. Although the hedge and roadside trees were planted less than twenty years ago a magical atmosphere has built up, the tree canopy has closed, suppressing the grass and weed growth and making it easy to walk along the shoulder of the embankment between the hedge and the slope down to the road about 30-40 yards below. Ash trees have dropped their yellow leaves brightening the "forest" floor and despite the noise of traffic there is a silence within this wooded cloister unfrequented by people.

18th
Saw a nuthatch in the backyard bury a beechnut in the crevice between paving slabs and then place leaves over the site. A second bird joined him and brought a nut to the bay tree pot by the back door of the house. The most amusing thing is the way they drive the nut home with a series of vertical blows of the beak like a pile driver.

19th
Paradise is always trying to re-establish itself – as soon as the cold showers die out and the sun comes out, once the tractor noise has died away and the farmer is in the house, a cat sleeps at the bottom of the stone farmhouse wall, underneath the cover of ivy in a bowl of leaves next to the base of a late flowering fuschia bush, fat smooth wood pigeons waddle about the paddock in front of the house, pecking at seeds.

20th
I walked around the back of the big shed and a blue/green/black dragonfly almost flew into my face. Only a last minute course adjustment on his part avoided a collision as he carried on his hurried way. Later a flock of geese could be heard a long time before they came into view high over the buildings – about twenty to thirty, winter must be on the way!

21st
Twenty four hours before the new moon it should have been very dark this morning at 5am and indeed the stars were very bright overhead but at ground level I was able to see more than usual because of a layer of frost reflecting what little light there was – it almost looked as if the fields were underlit.

22nd
What a sensual time autumn is – a time of alchemy. Dew gives way to frost, green to browns and gold. There is a row of young ash trees growing between our boundary hedge and the bypass. I have been noticing them change colour everyday – various yellows and the occasional reddish brown progressing to their autumnal conclusion. This morning in the 5am gloom looking along the length of the row was like being inside a dimly lit impressionist painting.

A very particular aspect of this for me is the colour of the hedges. We often cut a hedge at this time of year so there is plenty of opportunity to notice the reds and oranges of the berries, the special yellow that the hawthorn leaves become. Where there is alchemy there must be fire – the bonfire that consumes the thorns from hedgecutting. The ethereal smell of that pale blue smoke is very evocative, it is as distinctive as incense. I can pick it out instantly if it is carried here on the wind from anywhere in the valley. It is the perfect complement to the misty atmosphere on fine, dry October days.

23rd
The skylarks seem to prefer three of our fields on the shoulder of the slope down to the valley bottom. Just lately, whenever I move the electric fence I seem to disturb them, either singly or in a group. In the dark at 5.30 am it is not fair payment for their Maytime song! There is a new bird around, a snipe I think. It has long wings compared to its body, a white underside and longish beak. It flies away very fast when disturbed and zizzags on its path.

24th
A heron flew over the farmyard passing in front of the crescent moon in the south, a crow croaked its displeasure at the intruder.

25th
I have just seen a beautiful but eerie sight. Tonight there is just enough cloud to reflect the lights from Mold down in the valley. The big oak tree down the lane is catching this light and the entire canopy of leaves appears to be faintly luminous while the trunk and branches are a dark delicate network of shadow – a faery tree.

26th
The ash trees are festooned with their seeds – "keys" that hang from the semi bare branches in bunches, looking like roosting tropical bats.

27th
Wind and rain are playing havoc today. The wind has blown down a beech tree behind the house bringing down the power supply. I will be using the generator for the rest of today.

We have been lucky with the big oak tree down the lane. When I passed to bring the cows in from the field because of the bad weather it was okay but by the time I got back with the cows one of the biggest branches, almost a tree in itself had come down and blocked the lane. We had to turn the cows around and divert them across the field to get them in the yard. Only a few minutes earlier or later and the cows or myself might have been killed. It is only 10.30am and this storm has caused more damage for us than the big storm of 1987 which also brought a beech tree down but nothing more.

28th
A very close encounter with a badger – I was walking up the drive in the dark this evening when I heard a grunt and the scrape of claws on concrete, it was a large badger skidding to a halt to avoid running into me before turning and running back the way he came.

29th
I very much associate elderberries with the dark, with winter. I am currently picking a sprig each evening after dark, shining a torch up through the branches to choose a spray with the best berries. It is very pleasant to drink two

mugs of hot elderberry tea and go to bed feeling the warmth in the stomach, perhaps this rich, dark plant will give powerful dreams.

30th

I was finally able to sow the wheat yesterday, having been held up by the wet weather. Now the clocks have changed it is dark by 5.30pm which means that by the time the field is prepared we cannot finish sowing before dark.

Working in the dark on a tractor is a unique experience that perhaps can only be understood by others who have done it. There is no guidance of white lines and cats' eyes as when driving on roads at night so it is easy to get lost as to where you should be driving. There is only the arc of light from the headlights and the expanse of soil. Still I do not mind working late being glad of the chance to get the field sown. It might be wet again tomorrow. A heartening sight as dusk fell was the moon rising over the dingle that borders this field. Later on it threw its light on the harrows as I worked.

31st

Although an old pasture is less productive in a conventional sense I do like old grassland and the thought of the soil life beneath it. This is typified by the potash cycle fungus - the first year there is a circular ring of dark green grass where the fungus has mobilised potash and encouraged grass growth, the following year the same ring of grass is dead because it has had too much of that nutrient. This sort of thing is not seen in fertilised fields because the high amounts of nutrients suppresses the soil flora.

November

1st

The conditions are so good at the moment, so kind that I wish I could actually fabricate something out of them, weave something from the sunlight, the cool but drying breeze, the dry trackways with hundreds of acorns lying on them, the first yellowed leaves dropping, the mists and frost, the smell of bonfires, the hedgerow fruits....

2nd

I went to turn off the water supply to the field troughs and found a baby frog perched on top of the tap like a flood victim on his house roof because there was six inches of water in the bottom of the manhole. I rescued him and tightened the tap.

3rd

The winter landscape is beginning to establish itself now – the hedges have lost their leaves, the reds and oranges are giving way to the golds and browns of the oak trees that seem to shine so luminously in the few bursts of sunlight that make it past the slow moving towering banks of rain cloud.

4th
Very windy today, a constant stream of leaves are leaving the trees, an almost full moon rising in the east as I went to look at the cows.

5th
I was amused to see a crow walking along the edge of a pool of water standing in one of the fields after yesterday's rain. It was as if he was transformed into a waterfowl walking along bobbing his head up and down.

6th
I realised today that I must always have some larch trees somewhere – they shine bronze so wonderfully in the winter sunshine. There is a small tree behind the yard that I have considered felling in the past to make tractor manoeuvres more convenient, but having seen it this afternoon giving such a gift how could I ever repay it by cutting it down?

7th
After spending the morning dealing with a farm assurance inspection that meant paperwork and regulations it was a real pleasure to walk down the field to look at the cows, like stepping into a different world – a world of hazy November sunshine, of brown beech leaves blowing in ones and twos on the wind and skittering across the concrete lane. It would be almost possible to lose oneself in the ethereal fabric of that world and never return to paperwork!

8th
The aspens at the side of the drive were almost shimmering with a pale grey light from the moon as I walked past in the dark. The moonlight gave them an otherworldly quality, the leaves seeming to be opaque crystal.

9th
Even on a grey, damp, drizzly November day there is colour – a guelder rose on the edge of a ride in the wood has leaves that seem to glow from pink to yellow in its autumnal show.

10th
The lights of the town are illuminating the fog in the same way that the neon gas in a fluorescent tube glows. The last leaves of an oak tree are silhouetted against the eerie glow.

11th

I was delighted to see the regrowth on the hazel stools that I cut at the end of last winter. The rest of the wood is full of yellowed and brown leaves but the regrowth on the hazels is a strong vibrant green, the strong pliable shoots are 3 feet high. These little bushes exude the hope and vitality of regeneration.

12th

A collage of rectangular birch leaves evenly interspersed with larch needles, all yellows and browns and bronze on the wet drive.

13th

As I walked back to the house after looking round this evening I noticed the garden gate open and moonlight bathing the lawn beneath the monkey puzzle tree.

14th

Saw a badger on the farm drive tonight, waddling quickly to get off the concrete and out of sight.

15th

The leaves of the wild cherry trees are like flames in a fire, varying from red through to yellow. In a breeze they flutter almost horizontally like Buddhist prayer flags. Other trees have a pleasing mixture of yellowing leaves mixed with green, the oaks and larches (needles in their case) especially.

16th

At 5am the sky was clear with the Plough visible in the north and the waning moon shining in the south. Below that there was low level mist seeping through the farmyard. Everything was quiet, very quiet. As the sky lightened about 7am the bronze coloured larch and birch in the wood loomed tall above the pale mantle of mist. Later when the sun rose it illuminated the mist giving a soft focus to everything, contrasting with the almost electrical smell of the mist.

17th

Cutting back vegetation on the small island in the pond, I enjoyed the way that ripples from the slightest disturbance of the surface travelled right to the far end of the water.

18th
The weather has been very still for two days now, indeed I might say that there has been no weather so little is happening. The sky is grey, there is no breeze – the air is so still that the smoke from the chimney rises straight up in a vertical column for many feet until finally coiling around itself into a turban shape.

I was surprised to see five young hen pheasants together in the paddock, all speckled fawns and greys they slipped away, moving as one. Later on, at dinner time I saw a big cock pheasant sitting proudly on the top rail of the garden fence directly opposite the living room window. The hen pheasants (dare I say his hens?) were back also, feeding in the grass. I put out the weed seeds and broken grains that we clean out of the corn for them.

19th
Looking at one of the fields in the light of the low morning sunshine I noticed evenly spaced lines running up and down the slope. Are they old plough marks on a field that has not been ploughed in living memory?

20th
Frosty this morning, the hedges look as if they are powdered with icing sugar. When we worked in the wood later on there was a sound like gentle rain – it was the frost thawing off the canopy and dropping down through the leaves.

21st
Apparently the starling is or has been in decline recently but I have just seen the biggest flock of them that I have ever seen. Hundreds of them were massing on the hay field, landing in the grass to feed (I suppose) and disappearing because the grass was the same height as each individual bird then appearing again in one mass as they flew up, twisting and turning in their synchronised way before dropping down again out of sight. Each time they moved further along the field and it occurred to me that if I stopped where I was they might have surrounded me in a whirling vortex of flight. When I got back to the farmyard later they had moved to a field close by.

22nd
Saw a squirrel sitting upright on the bough of a dog rose eating a red hip held in his front claws.

23rd
When I drove into town this morning a river of leaves was flowing across the road by County Hall. The lay out of the land must have funnelled the wind a certain way causing it to carry the leaves in one continuous stream.

24th
It was frosty this morning and as the sun rose in the clear blue sky its rays touched only the tops of the trees at first colouring the brown leaves of an oak tree by the yard and gilding them a stunning bronze, as the sun climbed higher it illuminated the whole canopy making it shine like a giant paper lantern.

25th
The weather has been very pleasant today, the sunlight was playing on Moel Fammau and the banks of cloud around its peak, the air was clean and clear making the tree colours on the lower slopes stand out.

Although on a Saturday I try to have a couple of hours in the house after dinner this afternoon it was so nice outside I was reluctant to stay inside and was quite happy pottering around the yard doing oddjobs and watching the interplay of sunlight and cloud above.

As I write this it is dark but a half moon is illuminating the edges of the clouds making me wonder what it must be like up there above the vast fields of moonlit cloud moving gently along. It has been the sort of weather that leaves you thankful to whoever organises it.

26th
We have been collecting firewood in part of the wood where elderbushes form a complete understorey beneath the Scots pine and Douglas firs. There is no ground vegetation because of their dense growth which seems almost to form a forest of their own, not upright like the trees above but multistemmed, warped and sinister looking. How easy to believe that here in the shade they exude a dark narcotic influence on all around them.

As we work in the wood we cut back briars and low growing branches to make it easier to carry the firewood back to the trailer. The result of this is that paths open through the trees, not straight and planned but evolving according to the terrain, skirting trees, taking the best way across a slope or avoiding rabbit holes dug out by the dog (a hazard of tripping over). These paths vary from year to year like a river shifting its course across a flood plain.

27th
Sitting in the kitchen at coffee time I heard a tapping at the window of the back door. It was a coal tit pecking at the corner of the pane as it extracted an insect egg wrapped in floss and as the bird pulled at it the floss stretched and stretched and was obviously sticky, at one point he was swinging on the elasticated strand until finally it snapped and he got his prize. He was watched in all this by a companion and they then moved to the underside of the gutter on an outbuilding in the backyard. I was surprised to see them scavenging so close to the house this early in the winter, surely they have not exhausted food supplies out in the open countryside already.

28th
Despite the difficulties that hard frost causes us on the farm I cannot curse the winter - always some sight overcomes the trials. Today I saw an oak tree shedding a constant rain of leaves down through the frosty air while another tree had carpeted the cold concrete of the lane with yards and yards of crisp brown leaves.

29th
Because of the cold weather affecting the car starting I wanted to use an old horse blanket to cover the engine. This blanket has been hanging in the granary loft for years and as I pulled it off the beam there was a small screech. I could not at first see the cause until I found a small bodied bat on the floor stretching out its delicate wings. I hastily rehung the blanket, picked him up (not easy, how do you fold up bat wings?) and placed him back in his winter quarters to await the spring.

30th
There is a cock pheasant visiting the midden at the moment. He is quite tame, staying put while I walk past to get the post from the post box. He is very light coloured – his wings and tail are fawn, his head a greenish, blue purple with a white ring around his neck. But it is the chest that is his crowning glory – an almost paisley effect of mottled colours. All in all a very exotic looking bird to be scratching about on a farm midden.

December

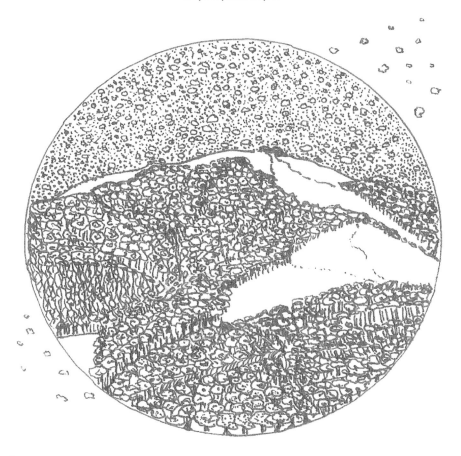

1st

The birds have eaten the flesh out of the windfall apples under the Bramley in the garden – managing to leave three quarters of the skin intact so that there are empty shells of apples left on the lawn. This morning I watched a moorhen pecking at the soft fermented flesh.

2nd

A pleasant sunny morning with mist lingering in places on the fields. I noticed the heifers that we had turned out for the day playing in a bank of knee deep mist that seemed to move with them as if they were dragging it across the field.

3rd

A pleasant morning with a mild breeze. I had to go into town for 7am and passed one of the cats sitting on the top of a fence post by the side of the drive and wondered what had he seen during the long night? In the town it was so dark it might have been midnight, the illuminated street lights only added to the illusion.

4th

A heron has started visiting the pond again since I cut back the vegetation on the island. I saw him this morning wheeling around as he came down to land and then stand sentinel on the pile of logs I have left as habitat.

5th

It was breezy but sunny when I took the dogs in the paddock this afternoon. I wandered over to look at the pond and found that the wind was moving the shining surface, sending ripples in all directions in such a way that it looked as if the water was welling up from unknown depths in the middle of the pond, the current moved to the right past the small island along the further bank and back to the centre then changed direction and circled back again. All the time the centre of the pond shone brightly, reflecting sunshine.

6th

It is still three nights until the full moon but it is very bright and the moon is so high in the sky it throws only a small shadow at my feet. Coming back from checking some cows at 9pm I passed my "singing" oak and sure enough I could hear the wind in her branches from forty yards away as I approached. How pleasant to think of her humming away underneath the moon and stars all night!

7th

I saw a strange sight as I walked up the drive between the two hedges tonight. It was dusk and there was a crowd of birds moving in a horizontal vortex between the hedges acting like starlings. I am sure the majority were blackbirds although when one bird broke off and alighted in the hedge nearer to me it was a young jay and there were smaller species such as robins and tits involved too. Blackbirds can be agitated at dusk but I have never seen so many together in one place and behaving in such a choreographed manner. Were they mobbing the jay?

8th
Looking at the silhouette of the ivy covered oak tree outside the yard gate in the predawn gloom I realized he looks like a shaggy giant wearing a furskin jerkin.

9th
After a clear day the air was very cold and at dusk the ridge of the Clwydian hills was outlined against a yellow glow that faded to blue, a crescent moon and star in the south.

10th
As I was shutting the door of the cubicle shed in the dark this morning I saw a sight that quite literally caused a sharp intake of breath. I had glanced towards the northwest and there was the moon setting over the wood. It appeared so large and close that from the cottage on the end of the wood it would have seemed as if it was sitting on the lawn beaming in through the window! But from my vantage point it sent up a fan of silver light, the lunar equivalent of a fine sunset but all in blacks, greys, silvers and whites.

11th
We are having a lot of fog recently. This morning the sun eventually shone in the upper layers, illuminating the cold grey air. Tonight the fog has returned, cutting us off from the outside world and the unearthly screech of barn owls adds to the eeriness.

12th
A little clearer today, but the bottom of the valley remained full of fog all day.

13th
Very windy all day. It blew a complete crows' nest out of the beech trees by the house, giving me the opportunity to study the structure of it – an untidy mass of twigs lined with mud, the "bowl" four inches deep. Well enough made to survive the drop of forty to fifty feet.

14th
Windy with showers this evening. At one point there was a shower of hail stones that hit the slate roof of a shed at 45 degrees and driven by the wind flowed up the slope and over the ridge tiles.

15th

It is now twenty years since we planted our first oak trees in the original wood. They have grown big enough to close their canopy, suppressing the vegetation growth at ground level. The leaves have dropped and the whole bare floor surface is one complete mosaic of oak leaves all pointing in different directions, looking like an autumnal William Morris design.

16th

As I passed the garden gate this morning I noticed the sun, so low in the south east that its rays were shining horizontally, illuminating the pale round "pennies" of the honesty seed pods still on the plants and making them glow like paper lanterns.

17th

In the stackyard there is a stump of an old lime tree that blew down years ago and then sent out new shoots which have themselves blown over. The original stump is covered in moss with cleavers and a thistle growing through it and some brown toadstools with round caps covered in small lumps that smooth out as the cap expands.

18th

9am. The air is clear and cold, just above freezing at 1C. The light seems to be striated – a golden layer at ground level as it passes horizontally through a filter of trees, oak leaves and larch needles before striking the yellowish stone of the farm buildings. Above these obstructions it is pure and clear.

19th

5.30am. The last sliver of moon was high in the sky with rain cloud beneath and as the cloud moved and billowed in the wind the moon illuminated the moving edges that seemed to form (literally) unearthly shapes and textures.

20th

A light covering of snow this morning. As I walked along the drive to check that the milk tanker could get up the slope the sun was shining and the sky was blue but I could see another band of snow coming down the valley, a grey cloud much more substantial than a rain cloud and as the leading edge moved across the fields and trees they turned grey and black before being obliterated from view by the enveloping bank of grey. Very soon it reached me and flurries of wet snow and sleet fell from the now grey sky, the sun having disappeared.

By now I was returning to the yard through the woods and noticed how the larch branches overhang the track, their seed cones dark brown against the light brown branches and one or two clusters of guelder rose berries adding some red – natural baubles and Christmas tree decorations!

21st
Today has been very fitting for the winter solstice. It has been a day of cold fog that almost felt like drizzle and obscured the sun so much that it started to go dark by 3.30pm.

I was up at 1am to calve one of our oldest cows – she has had ten calves but is as pleased with her new born as any first time heifer. It is always heartening to see a cow's first reaction to her calf, one of the highlights of the job that makes it worth getting up at that ungodly hour!

22nd
"Red sky in the morning" reflected on the surface of the pond.

23rd
A freezing fog has descended on the world, blotting out everything and cutting us off from the rest of the valley. It has crept inside everywhere, dampening the hay safe inside the hay shed and leaving drops of moisture on the bare hawthorn branches. The edge of visibility is marked by trees vaguely discernable, their topmost branches swaying in the cold breeze.

24th
Went to the wood to get a Christmas tree and straight away I felt that I do not go there enough – I so appreciate the atmosphere of the trees, despite the litter from the lay-by and the glass jars, bottles and even light bulbs dug up by badgers from the council refuse tipped and buried here in the fifties. Even though most of the trees have only been planted since then there is a sylvan charm in this three acre plot. When I got to the conifer part of the wood I saw that a fern had established itself half way down the slope to the stream and was now large enough to give a tropical feel to that spot. The glossy spears of Lords and Ladies are starting into growth and hint of the spring to come.

25th
Moel Fammau looked magnificent as I walked up the drive this morning. The air was cold and clear, increasing visibility and making the mountain appear

closer than usual. There was a slight sprinkling of snow on the summit and shoulders which served to pick out and enhance the folds of the slopes. The forest was like a shawl thrown around her ancient shoulders.

26th
This morning clouds or a snowstorm were moving around the mountain almost as if it was swirling them around itself. Five minutes later the summit was visible, the clouds gone. It was strange how such a great volume of matter, thousands of cubic feet of vapour or snow that made up the clouds can apparently disappear.

A pair of buzzards wheeled and mewed above the field.

27th
The weather is quite frosty at the moment, there has been a covering of half an inch of snow on the ground for three days and each night the temperature drops to about -1C.

We have been invaded by lapwings with ten to twenty of them standing in each field, heads up and alert, equidistant from each other. I suppose the hard weather has driven them here from their normal grounds.

I saw a bird standing on the frozen pond, when I went closer to look it was a heron that flapped so wearily away that I regretted intruding.

28th
5.30am. A crescent moon and planet rising in the south east over a band of purple in the predawn sky. The stone farm buildings silhouetted against the gloaming, a slight mist in the lane, it is -2.5C.

Later, a very fat wood pigeon forages on the surface of a straw bale in the afternoon sunlight, framed by the roof, uprights and wall of the barn.

29th
A cold, clear starry morning when I went out to milk. As the sky lightened in the east the stars disappeared apart from one or two of the brightest that lingered on, at one point it seemed that the firmament was divided – one half still dark and starry and the other lightening into day.

30th
Very dark this morning, it's hard to believe that we are over a week past the solstice. It has been very wet overnight. There was a large puddle in the yard due to a blocked grid when I went out to milk. Once it went dark this evening however it was more pleasant than it had been all day, breezy but the moonlight made the wet roofs shine.

31st
The moon is shining as Orion rises above the trees behind the house tonight.

Lightning Source UK Ltd.
Milton Keynes UK
UKOW06f0603070316

269735UK00007B/74/P